# THE DIRT ROAD
# TO SUCCESS

# THE DIRT ROAD
# TO SUCCESS

Proven strategies for navigating
the rough trails of life and business

## Brian Fisher

## Fisher's ATV World, LTD.

ISBN-13: 978-1508822677  ISBN-10: 1508822670

Printed in the United States of America.

*To my mother Alma Breach for*

*Inspiring me to dream and*

*to my father William P. Breach*

*for always believing in me.*

# CONTENTS

# PREFACE

Brian Fisher's journey to becoming a national television host and business owner extraordinaire is an incredible success story—one of true endurance that applies to many people on their dirt road to business success. Let his dark horse story encourage and inspire you as he travels bumpy roads, twists, and turns and faces challenges and adversities along the way.

Brian knows what it takes to be successful. In *The Dirt Road to Success* he shares what he has learned and offers hands-on and proven lessons—the real deal— to help you navigate the rough trails of becoming the best you can be in life and in business.

Some of what you'll read in this book, you've probably heard already. But maybe you weren't ready for it then and it didn't hit home. Maybe you're still not ready. People go through different phases in life at their own speed. Sometimes you need to hear things over and over before you take it to heart. Certain parts of this book will be more meaningful to you because of where you are in your life.

## What Is Success to You?

Everyone's definition of success is different. It's not always about money or what job you have. It could be as simple as being a good parent, making a good living, loving your occupation, having more time to do what makes you happy or enough money to retire comfortably. Only you can determine what success is to you.

One way to move forward is NEVER let yourself get too comfortable. Build on your strengths and talents to design your life the way you want it to be. That's exactly what Brian did!

## The Dirt Road to Success: The Success and Pitfalls of Being an Entrepreneur

Brian shares the principles, strengths, and resilience factors that powered him through challenge and adversity to build an incredible life and prosperous business. In *The Dirt Road to Success*, you'll get practical information to help power you through challenges on your own uphill and possibly muddy dirt road.

Learn how Brian built several successful businesses utilizing three important keys: Stay Focused, Go Beyond Average, and Be Persistent. His "dirt road story" offers firsthand experiences and knowledge to lead you to true triumph. You'll take away ideas to apply to your business right away and most importantly, the kick in the pants you may need to get you moving!

## Building a Booming Business with Your Spouse: The "Home Team" Advantage in Business

They say friends and family are the hardest to work with. If that's true, then building a successful business with your spouse should be nearly impossible. Brian Fisher and his wife Melissa are an exception to this rule; they've been chasing their dreams together since 1987 and are still going strong. With Brian's real-world stories of turning challenge and even adversity into opportunity, you'll learn the secrets and principles to building a booming business with your spouse while maintaining a great relationship.

Brian and Melissa have built their empire from literally nothing. They've mastered the work/life balance, while raising three children and continually striving toward the next goal. Brian teaches the principles and standards they shared to push them through every challenge and hardship, creating an even stronger relationship and team. The *Dirt Road to Success* hands you lots of ideas to apply in creating your own dream team.

# ACKNOWLEDGMENTS

First and foremost, I would like to thank my wife Melissa for always believing in me and sharing the same passion for accomplishing our goals and dreams. She is not only my best friend and business partner but more so, my rock and soul mate. My story wouldn't have the fairy tale ending without her and for that I am extremely grateful. I would also like to thank our three children: Tyler, Briana, and Brady for traveling the dirt road with us and experiencing the hard work and sacrifices we've made to reach our destination. I hope our journey taught you all that life is what you make it!

# CHAPTER 1

## 236 Out of 236: The Dirt Road to Success (Removing Labels & Negative People)

I was lost for many years. I know there are plenty of people in that same position. I always had a burn deep down inside me that I wanted more out of life; however, any time I let a little of it out, someone around me would shut me down, telling me I needed to be more realistic and quit dreaming. They were always quick to remind me that I was a terrible student with a bad attitude; I didn't have a clue about the real world and how it works, and so on. It doesn't take long before you begin to think that there *is* something wrong with you because you don't see life the way everybody else does.

As time went on, I became really intrigued with successful people. I started to educate myself about what made these people so different. How did they go on to achieve so many great things in their lives? The first thing that stood out is that many of these super-successful people started out right where I was—lost and wanting more. I devoted a lot of time looking for that one major key to success and after years of research, I discovered that there are many keys to success. My educational journey helped me understand that I could *do*, *have*, or *be* anything I put my mind to. This idea opened up a whole new world for me.

Looking back over my life and putting it into perspective, I've narrowed the success I've experienced to three major keys that propelled us through challenge and even adversity time and time again. No matter where you are in your life right now, from unemployed to CEO, you can take something away from *The Dirt Road to Success* that will change your life if you apply it.

If you're comfortable, you may not get anything at all out of this book. Am I saying this is a get rich quick manual? Absolutely not and if that's what you're looking for, you need not read any further. When you are ready to commit to the work it will take, you will achieve balance in your life. If you're thinking, *I'm not looking for balance. I'm looking to make more money and have a better life*, then, believe me; balance is just what you're looking for.

I have always been a huge believer in "If you haven't done it, how can you teach others how to do it?" I take advice from people who have done what I want to do and experienced a level of success at it. The world is full of people who will tell you how it should be done, but if they haven't done anything except research, why should you listen to them?

Here's a good analogy that I like to use: Let's say you're on a plane flying at 30,000 feet and the flight attendant holds up a briefcase and says "We just found a bomb on board and we only have five minutes to disarm it or we will all die. Does anyone here know how to disarm a bomb?" One guy stands up and says, "I've read all about it, even watched a lot of You Tube videos on disarming a bomb. I think I can do it." Another guy stands up and says, "I've disarmed over one hundred of those in the army. I can do it." Who are you going to go with—the guy who's only read about it and watched instructional videos or the guy who's actually done it?

People ask me all the time, "How did you do it?" My goal in writing this book and sharing my dirt road story is to help as many people as possible determine what success is to them and to accomplish everything they want out of their business and their life. If I can do it, so can you!

If something really strikes you or sticks in your mind as you read *The Dirt Road to Success*, I encourage you to use a highlighter and pen to make notes inside the book so you can easily reference that exact material. Think of this as a workbook and make it yours. I do this all the time because I read a lot and don't have time to go back through each and every book searching for the bit that I found most useful.

If you are hungry and are willing to apply what you learn from my personal experiences, you can get your life and business moving in the right direction!

## From the Beginning

I was born May 27, 1968, in York, Pennsylvania to Linda Breach —a single mother who passed away in a car accident when I was only ten months old. I grew up in the small town of Dover, Pennsylvania, where my grandparents, Bill and Alma Breach, raised me. I knew them as Dad and Mom. They were both in their fifties when I was born and had already raised three kids, so it was like starting over for them.

I don't think school and sports were a high priority to either of my parents at this point, so needless to say, I wasn't the best student. Truthfully, I did just barely enough to get by. I was not very tall so I got picked on a lot in grade school. I remember coming home after getting in fights on the bus and having my shirt ripped up. Finally, one day my dad told me it was time to stand up for myself and that's exactly what I did. A week later I broke a kid's nose for picking on me on the school bus. It wasn't long before his dad showed up at our front door and I overheard my dad telling him that his son was a bully and deserved what he got.

## A Good Education

When I was in fourth grade, my parents and teachers held me back because they thought my grades should be better. By my second tour of fourth grade, my teachers had started to label me. At one point, my fourth-grade math teacher snapped in front of the whole class and said, "Brian Fisher, you're nothing but a bum and that's all you'll ever be." She must have been pretty serious about that, too, because she used my full name—all because I didn't know the answer to her question.

My entire school career from K–12 was a nightmare for me. I hated school with a passion. I was focused on where I wanted to be, what I wanted to do, and what business I wanted to own. It only got worse as I got older. I remember in high school a teacher said, "Mr. Fisher, I don't even know why you show up for my class. All you do is hold everyone else back. You're nothing but a waste of time. You'll never be anything in life." I became the topic of conversation in the teacher's faculty rooms. Countless times teachers told me that I was a bum and never going to amount to anything.

I may not have been the smartest kid in school, but I sensed that they were all pretty miserable with their lives. None of them were dressing the way I wanted to dress, driving the cars I wanted to drive, living in the house I wanted to live in, or living the kind of lifestyle I wanted to live, so their opinions were completely irrelevant to me.

During my senior year, I had my system down on how to get out of school and get credit for being there without getting written up. I had a full time job, and school just didn't seem that important to me. I pushed myself to get through to graduation and was ranked 236 out of 236 in my senior class—yes, the very bottom of my class. This is something I am not proud of. If I could go back and do it over, would I have paid more attention and done better in school? Absolutely!

Now that I am older, I realize that a good education is important but I've seen countless times where a good education is no guarantee that you will be successful. You could have more degrees than a thermometer but if you don't have the hunger, drive, and discipline, that education won't get you very far.

## Where Do I Fit In?

Many of my peers were caught up in a lot of bad stuff like drugs and alcohol but I wasn't one of them. Actually, I never used drugs and waited until I was twenty-three years old before I had my first beer. Now don't get me wrong; I was certainly no perfect angel. I was always up for raising hell, throwing down in a good fight, and racing and even outrunning cops in my Mustang GT, but for the most part, my life was on the straight and narrow. I kept my distance from people and was sort of withdrawn dealing with the struggle of trying to figure out where I fit in. I never fell into the peer pressure trap because I didn't really care what other people thought.

I always had a goal to own my own business and that was the one thing that kept me going. Goals or dreams are the motivation that keeps us all moving forward. My story proves that you can do anything you want to do if you put your mind to it and are willing to work to get it.

## Don't Listen to the Critics

I had a lot of labels to remove by the time I graduated from high school. If I had let any of those teacher's opinions of me become my reality, I wouldn't have the life I have today. You'll always have critics—people who think they know everything—and negative people telling you that you can't do it, it won't work, or it is impossible. Truthfully, they probably don't want you to make it because they want you to stay on the same level or below them. That's a comfort zone for most people around you.

Generally, you are like the people you associate with. That's a hard reality. If you take a look at your five closest friends, you more than likely act like them, dress like them, fall into the same income bracket, and so on. You might want to evaluate your friendship circle and surround yourself with people you want to be like and who are where you want to be.

It amazes me how many people let themselves be held back from accomplishing big things in their lives because they listen to what other people think. Family and friends are often the biggest critics telling you why you can't or shouldn't do something. Negative people are like a cancer that will eat you alive. Don't feed into this by saying negative things about yourself. There are plenty of other people out there willing to do that for you. Dwelling on negative brings down everything you are and everything you are trying to accomplish. Let those negative people motivate you. If they laugh at you and make you uncomfortable, let that drive you! Work to reach your goals and dreams and then make them eat a s#!+ sandwich with no bread!

Is there someone in your life who has doubted you or laughed at you? Maybe this individual put you down and tried everything to hold you back? That person or group of friends can help push you forward because you want so much to prove them wrong. When you don't feel like doing something for yourself or your business, you can always find the energy and drive if you let the opinion or words of your enemy or nemesis motivate you.

After a few years on television, one of my high school teachers saw our office administrator and told her that he feels he owes me an apology. He said, "Brian proved that you can't judge a book by its cover." This just reinforces the theory of multiple intelligences written by Howard Gardner—"It's not how smart you are. It's how you are smart."

## Control Your Surroundings

You need to surround yourself with good, positive people and things that make you happy. Take advice and listen to people who are where you want to be— not relatives and neighbors that just think they know everything. They will be the first to tell you that you can't do it! Whatever you tell yourself, you're going to believe. The best part about it is that this is something you can control.

Another way of avoiding the negative is not to get wrapped up with constantly airing things on social media. Prospective employers, other businesses, partners, management, schools, and so on use these sites as tools to obtain background info and check you out. I know we always did when hiring someone or researching a company we were doing business with. You should always use discretion with your content and/or images on any social sites. Your reputation is at stake, and your direction in life can change in an instant because of one lapse in judgment.

## A Fresh Start

Did you ever wish you could start over? Well every day is a new day for a fresh start. You probably know what happened yesterday, last week, or even last year, but do you know what's going to happen tomorrow? Neither do I. To me, it is so exciting to know that I'm in total control of whether I better myself, work harder, strengthen my relationship with my family, make new friendships, and do whatever it takes to progress in my business. Some people start their week with, "OMG, It's Monday." It's all in how you look at it. You bet its Monday! It's a new week and a perfect opportunity to work on your goals, getting you one step closer to your dreams.

Where you are in life is a reflection of what you've done every day leading up to today. Your life story is unique and it's all because of you, not someone else or what someone has done to you. It's so easy to point your finger and blame someone else. The first thing you need to do is take 100 percent responsibility for your life and your actions. Most people don't have the discipline to do what they need to do, to live the kind of life they want to live.

A great starting point to put yourself on the right track is to take a look at your life and think seriously about all the things you are thankful for. It could be your health, your family, your kids, or a car; whatever makes you feel truly blessed. Everyone, no matter how down and out they are, can find some things to be grateful for. That is your starting line.

# CHAPTER 2

## Set Your GPS for YOUR Destination! (Goals & Dreams)

Most people take more time planning a family vacation or a summer party than they do planning their life. Are you doing what you want to do for a living? Close your eyes and picture yourself where you want to be in the next two, five, ten or twenty years. You need to design your life and figure out exactly where you want to be. Then you can figure out how you will get there. It's more important to have your "why" first. You don't just jump in the car and start driving without a destination in mind, do you?

Where you are now is just your location, not your destination. Your destination (or goal) is where you are going and what you are working or moving toward. Think of your brain as your personal computer, your internal GPS. It will do what you program it to do.

Your brain doesn't know the difference between reality and a dream. What you think about, envision, and work toward is what your brain will believe and will work to achieve.

Build your life plan first, and then build your business plan. Planning my life wasn't something that was high on my priority list, but when I started, it made a huge difference in the direction my life was moving.

## Write It Down and Visualize

The first thing I recommend that you do is show commitment to your goals by writing them out. Really think about what you want to accomplish, as you put your pen to paper and write at least three thirty-day goals, three sixty-day goals, and three ninety-day goals. These are the short-term goals needed for change and to get you moving forward toward accomplishing your long-term goals. When you've finished that, start thinking about and writing your personal goals for one year, five years, ten years, and even a twenty-five-year goal.

Don't be afraid to think BIG as you set your goals. Your brain will work to push you in that direction. This is all part of the law of attraction. You'll actually be drawn to the people, connections, and finances you need in order to make your goals/dreams and lifestyle a reality. This is no joke! I have done this more times than I can count.

The law of attraction (LOA) is a theory that many successful people attribute to their achievements.

What you see, you will believe. If you want to win a race, see yourself winning the race. If you want to lose weight, see yourself losing weight.

Give each of your goals specific details too. If it's a car—what year, make, model, color, and so on? Get pictures and put them in front of you. Hang them on your bathroom mirror or computer desktop, put a picture in your vehicle, day planner, smartphone, or tablet, anywhere you look every day. These pictures will serve as reminders. The more you see your goals and are reminded of them, the more progress you can make. The small attainable goals will help you get to your larger goal. The best feeling in the world is when you've been busting your ass for something and start to see results.

When you hit a roadblock and start getting discouraged and questioning yourself, your "why" will inspire you to push on. The more detailed it is, the easier it will be for you to stay on track and move forward when you meet challenges or setbacks.

You will achieve what your mind conceives! That is exactly why you need to speak it into existence. What you tell yourself, you will believe. If you tell yourself you're fat, you'll more than likely be fat. If you tell yourself you're poor, you'll more than likely be poor.

Start reprogramming your brain so that you can see yourself where you want to be.

## The Dream Team Begins

I always knew I wanted to have my own business but another goal I had was to find the right person, settle down, and create a good family life. I met Melissa a couple months after I graduated. I don't want to sound hokey, but I knew when I saw her for the first time that she was the one. I actually met her through a mutual friend. I wound up asking her for a ride because I had fallen asleep, after working a lot of overtime at my full-time job, and crashed my Mustang GT into the living room of a house. Everything happens for a reason, right?

I used to take Melissa up to our local lake and we would just sit there under the stars and dream about our future. What would it be like? Where would we live? Who would our friends be? What would our children be like? What kind of car would we drive? We talked about and imagined everything.

Neither of us chose to go to college possibly because we didn't come from a background that would have pushed us to do so. I got a job at a printing company, which I kept for twelve years. Melissa was working in payroll at a roofing company when I met her, but she later got a position as a paralegal, which she held for the next five years.

## A Rough Foundation

The first five years of our relationship was kind of rocky because we were both strong willed. I was a total introvert and didn't like being around people, and she was the complete opposite. If there was a party or social gathering, she was there. One of my favorite hobbies was deer hunting. This was probably because it was something I could do all by myself. I spent many hours in the tree stand alone, which is where I was most comfortable.

We went about life kind of backward and bought our first house together about three years into our relationship, before we got married. We had a lot of disagreements, probably more than anyone I've ever known. There were many days when we both wondered if we'd made the right decision.

I will never forget how I felt when I came home from work one day to an empty house. We'd had yet another disagreement, but this time she left and took everything but the salt-and-pepper shakers. I thought we had been robbed! It had taken us a week to move into the house, but it only took her and a couple of girlfriends a few hours to move everything out. That moment was a real game changer because I knew if I wanted her back, I needed to make some changes.

I kept after her to come back but all I was doing was pushing her away. For the first month, I kept calling her, stalking her, and telling her I was going to change. Nothing worked. I was lonely and depressed and took to drinking a lot of alcohol.

I recall waking up alone on Christmas morning and seeing my nickel-plated 357 Magnum with an 8-inch barrel lying beside me. This gun looked like something right out of a Dirty Harry movie. I have no idea how it got there because I had been drinking heavily the night before just trying to drown the pain. But waking up with that gun scared me enough to make me realize that it was time for a new direction. As soon as I saw it, I said to myself, "It's time to get your shit together Fisher." That's when I started working on myself, living my own life, and leaving her alone.

## New Directions and Change

After about a month or two of this, Melissa was starting to notice a difference in me because I wasn't bugging her anymore. I started to socialize more and surround myself with friends. It wasn't long before we started talking again and rediscovered the friendship that had started our whole relationship to begin with. She moved back into our house and we got married that same year.

After our first child was born, we decided we wanted Melissa at home raising our children, so she quit her job at the law office. That drastically reduced our income, but we were willing to make that sacrifice. It wasn't easy living on one income. As I mentioned, I worked at a printing company full time for twelve years with as much overtime as I could get, and it still never seemed to be enough. To get the hours, I worked twelve-hour swing shifts, weekends, holidays, and stayed on call all the time.

## Survival Mode

My goal in those early years of family life was to just have a full tank of gas in my vehicle and to have a $5 bill in my pocket. We were in survival mode for quite some time, just trying to keep bread, milk, and eggs in the house for the kids. I used to crawl under the vending machines at work to scrape up change that was dropped so I could buy a soda. But then I couldn't bring myself to buy it because I knew Melissa and the kids couldn't have one.

My transportation to work was a twenty-minute car. It had a blown head gasket, which meant I had twenty minutes to drive before it overheated. That's about how long it took me to get to work. This car didn't have a working heater and we lived in Pennsylvania, so driving to work in the winter was a challenge. That was just one of the piece of junks we drove then. Believe me, there were many more to follow.

Not having enough money to make a decent living was not my idea of a happy life. We fell behind on many of our bills and the bank almost foreclosed on our house. Fortunately, we sold it one week before they came to take it back. It is amazing how much stress and strain finances can put on a relationship. We know and understand that struggle personally because we fought our way through it.

I recall a survival moment that hit me hard and is still one of the main reasons I work so relentlessly. My son Tyler (who was only four years old at the time) and I were at the mall helping my dad and mom load out from a holiday flower stand they had set up in the middle of the mall. As we were walking out of the mall hand in hand, Tyler asked if he could have a soft pretzel. I just kept walking and told him "Maybe next time buddy."

The pretzel was only 35¢, but the sick part was I didn't have 35¢ to my name. I didn't tell Tyler that, and he didn't really seem to care that he wasn't getting a pretzel. When we got to our vehicle, I put him in the car seat and walked around to the other side and said to myself, "that will never happen again." At that very moment, my dream/goal became clearer than it had ever been before. I wanted to be a better provider to take care of my family.

## Our First Business Together

As we were trying to find our place in the world as a family, we got involved in a multilevel marketing (MLM) or networking business for about three years. This was our first attempt at a business together and we became successful in a short period of time, which was rewarding. This level of success required us to attend a lot of functions and meetings that took extra travel money we didn't really have, but we came up with it somehow. Fortunately, my dad and mom and Melissa's mom really helped us out by watching our kids when we needed them to as we pursued our dreams.

During that time, I made a major sacrifice by taking a demotion at my printing company job to basically become a janitor. This offered normal working hours so that my evenings would be free to do meetings. I knew that nothing would change for us until we made a change, so we were willing to do whatever it took.

Those years were definitely the beginning of big changes in our life as we started communicating, dreaming, and setting goals together. We read tons of self-help books and attended a lot of business/motivational speaking seminars, which helped us grow both on a personal level and a business level.

After a few years with some success in the MLM business, Melissa and I were thinking it might be time to move on. We just weren't sure we wanted to let that business go. I was reading a book called *Feel the Fear and Do It Anyway* by Susan Jeffers and came across a valuable quote: "If you're not happy doing what you're doing, it's okay to change direction and do something else. That doesn't mean you're a loser. It just means that you want to do something else." Shortly after that we made the decision to move on from the MLM business. While the MLM business changed our life for the better, it wasn't where my GPS was set.

## Sharing Our Dreams

We used to drive by dream homes near our neighborhood and test-drive new cars. Even though we haven't achieved everything we dreamed of yet, this was something we could see, feel, and touch that kept our goals fresh in our minds. These items wouldn't exist if people weren't able to buy them. Why not for us? I've always felt that we were all created equal and given many of the same opportunities in life.

Having goals and dreams are an important part of life. Your definition of success isn't the same as other people's definition, and that makes us all unique. There are three characteristics of highly successful, truly happy people: progress, purpose, and giving back. These are all essential traits to leading a fulfilling successful life.

My dream was to be a good husband and father and be able to provide for my family. I also wanted to help other people live a more fulfilling life. Some people say money isn't everything, which is true, but it is a tool that helps balance most things in your life—your needs for your life and the people you care about. According to Volunteers of America (voa.org), there are over 670,000 people who are homeless in America and 48 million people who go hungry every night. Did you know that 46.2 million people live in poverty in America? With numbers like that, you can bet there is always someone in desperate need of help.

When I'm on the road meeting people, they usually ask me, "Did you ever see yourself doing this or becoming successful?" My simple answer is yes because I did envision my life this way. I've always been a big dreamer, which often scared my wife. I would tell her things we were going to be doing, places we were going to visit, and people we were going to hang out with and she would just shake her head as if to tell me "Okay, whatever" but she never discouraged me. The craziest thing is that most of those things I told her from the beginning have already come true. See yourself where you want to be.

Being successful does not happen by accident! You need to envision it and be willing to work your ass off for it! It will not be easy and that's exactly why most people are not successful. It's about creating your own opportunities because we all know it's not going to come to you. You have to go after it. That's what life is all about. Our team motto: We "MSH" or We Make S#!+ Happen!

## The Right Direction

A dream without a plan is just a wish. The difference? A wish will drift away but a dream will keep coming back to you, over and over again. Once you know what you want, then it's time to figure out your "how." Consider this your vehicle. It's time to shift it into gear and drive. You begin your trip by making small destinations (or goals) that will lead into larger destinations/goals. If you have a road map for where you're heading and for what you want out of life, you will start attracting the people and opportunities to make it happen.

Don't wait to get started on pursuing your dreams and reaching your goals! This is not a New Year's Resolution or I'll start tomorrow or Monday. Procrastination is a killer. You need to start today! No matter what you want to do or change, it's what you do every day that will get you where you want to be. Nothing will happen overnight but with persistence, anything is possible.

Always look where you are heading, not where you're at now. It is okay to reflect back on where you came from but don't focus on it. Focus on where you want to be. That's why you have a huge windshield in your vehicle, so you can see where you are going. Your rear view mirror is much smaller than your windshield because it's more important to see what's up ahead, rather than what's behind you.

When you program your GPS for a destination and come up against a detour or wrong turn, what happens? The GPS reroutes you so that you still get where you were going, but it might take a little longer. This same thing happens in life and business. When you come up against a detour or wrong turn, you need to stay focused and find a way around it, over it, under it, or through it to get to your destination.

# CHAPTER 3

## Following a Narrow Path:
## Staying Focused

A lot of people spend their lives looking for the secret to success, when the answer is usually right in front of them. The problem is, most people don't like that answer and they keep looking for something easier. They don't want to have to work so hard. The answer? Commit to whatever it is that you want and sell out! If you want to make more money, put yourself in a position to do that. Maybe you don't have the right vehicle (career) to get you where you want to be financially or maybe you do have the right vehicle and opportunities but just aren't working hard enough to reach your goal. You need to get a clear focus on what you want and go after it, with no looking back. There is no Plan B. You need to stay focused on Plan A and see it through.

### Too Many Business Ideas

Staying focused was one of the hardest things for me to do. I think I had ADD before this was something that was commonly diagnosed. If I didn't see results right away, I would quit that business or idea and move on to the next one. Maybe that was part of the reason we quit the MLM business, I don't know. I've tried many different businesses over the years mainly because I couldn't stay focused. Possibly we just had to find our niche. I got discouraged. I still remember sitting out in back of our house on the picnic table with my head hung low telling Melissa that I was depressed because I didn't know what I was going to do. It seemed like I had run out of "great" ideas.

One of my very last attempts at a "part-time" business was selling used cars and trucks out of my front yard. Everyone had us selling their vehicles and we were pretty good at it, until we got a notice from the Department of Transportation (DOT) telling us that we needed a business license and a legit place of business in order to sell any more vehicles there. Now what?

## A Possible Big Break

My next big idea? Write a book and put together a used car kit complete with everything you need to sell your own used vehicles. Once we completed the book and got the package together, I decided I would take it to a local multimillionaire in our area with hopes that he might have some interest in investing and helping me get it launched.

The only reason I had this gentleman's contact information was because his house had a place on our dream list and Melissa and I would drive by it each week. One day he saw us driving by and stopped us to see what we were up to because we were in a private cul-de-sac. We had a good conversation about dreams and goals, which eventually led to him inviting us in to look around. He and his wife were so friendly and their home was just as incredible inside as it was outside. I believe the only reason he took the meeting on my used car sales kit was because he felt sorry for me.

I set up the meeting and went in with the sales package in my briefcase thinking this could be my break. The meeting went well but as I went to pull the sales package out of my briefcase, he held up his hand as if to say *stop* and said, "I don't even want to see what you have." I was devastated. He didn't even want me to show it to him or even talk about it. For the next two and a half hours, I just listened with an open mind as he talked to me about staying focused. At the time, I didn't really understand, but that simple advice has changed my life forever.

*Key #1: Stay Focused! I attribute much of my success to this one simple key in business.*

After watching all kinds of get-rich-quick schemes and real estate infomercials, I finally came to the conclusion that I wanted to do something I truly enjoyed. We were good at sales. So good that DOT came in and shut us down earlier in the year. If we could do something with sales, I thought we might just be onto something.

## Building Something from Nothing

My family and I have always enjoyed riding all-terrain vehicles (ATVs) and spending time outdoors, so we decided to begin selling ATVs from our front yard. This had nothing to do with DOT. The ATV industry was on the verge of exploding and we were ready to roll the dice again.

In the spring of 1998, Melissa and I started an ATV business and we were ready to give it 100 percent of our focus. Now when I say we started an ATV business, we literally didn't have anything to get started with. We didn't even have a business plan or mission statement. The banks all laughed at us and told us we would never make it past six months.

My next resource was a high-interest loan at a smaller bank. The day we went for the loan rain was pouring down. When we got there, I parked in the first parking spot nearest the front door with the passenger's side facing the bank's door and the driver's side out of view. I did this because the right side looked awesome, especially in the rain, and the left side was all rusted out and looked like crap. The loan officer looked out the door at our Jeep and said, "It looks pretty good from here. You mind if I don't go out and look at it since it's raining?" I said, "That's cool with me!"

As we were sitting down to sign the papers, Melissa was crying because she knew we were just getting deeper and deeper in debt. I'm sure she had every right to be upset because we had tried every other business and had now quit to go in a different direction. This was all while I maintained my full-time job at the printing company. I'm sure she thought *what's going to be different about this one*? The loan we took out was a 28 percent interest loan. When the loan officer came in and sat down with us, he said, "I'll give you $5,000, and you give me the title to your Jeep as collateral." I said, "You bet." I didn't want to tell him that our Jeep wasn't worth $1,500 but we took the money and we were off to start our dealership.

The first two ATVs I bought were a 1992 Honda TRX 250 and a 1987 Kawasaki Mojave. They needed a little work, so I fixed and cleaned them up and set them in our front yard for sale. Within an hour, we sold both and made $5,000 profit, which was enough to pay back the high-interest loan. Instead of paying the loan off, we used that money to buy more and kept reinvesting until eventually we had anywhere from six to eight ATVs sitting along the road. Soon, we knew it was time to open a dealership because at any given time, we would have three to four cars parked in front of our house because people wanted to see what we had for sale.

## Reinvesting Time and Money

Melissa and I opened our dealership—Fisher's ATV World—in October 1999 and put all the cash we had into opening the doors. We had no idea how much money it took to start a dealership and invested most of our cash just getting everything set up. Our inventory was back down to two used ATVs again. That first month we had an open house with those two ATVs on the floor. Customers would come in and say, "I thought this was a dealership" and we would tell them, "You come back next week, we'll have oil." So they would come back and we would have oil.

We took the advice our business friend gave us and stayed focused on building our dealership. Each week we would add something more to our store until eventually all our shelves were filled. This took some time because we didn't take out a loan to fill the shelves. Instead, we took the money we made and reinvested it back into our business to keep things going.

I had to travel a few hours each week to pick up the ATVs that we were selling at our dealership. My old truck didn't have heat, but at that point I only used it for picking up the ATVs we would sell, so I dealt with it.

## Doing Whatever It Takes

One cold winter morning I was on my way to New York, which was five hours one way, to pick up a few ATVs from a dealer. When I got about fifteen minutes away from our ATV dealership, the entire exhaust fell off my truck from the cab back. I pulled over and took a look underneath and then stood there in disbelief and contemplated turning around. I knew we had bills to pay and we relied on this money so I picked up my exhaust, threw it into the bed of my truck, and got back in and kept on going. It is in times like this that knowing your "why" will keep you pushing forward.

That ride to New York was so cold, and the exhaust was so loud and stinky the whole way there and back. I could have literally died from carbon monoxide that night. It wasn't the smartest thing to do but I got it done. It would have been so easy to turn around, go back home, and give up. But there was money to be made and I was on a mission, so I had to stay focused. Our tenacity pushed us through times like this. We were always willing to do what most others were not, which is a definitive quality of a truly successful person.

## Competition Is a Good Thing

We had a few large powersports dealers within thirty minutes of our dealership when we opened the doors. They were very competitive but in dealing with them before, we knew they lacked good customer service. We heard through the grapevine that they thought we were no threat to their business because we were so small and only selling used ATVs. They were just more critics as far as we were concerned. They had no idea who we were but it didn't take long for them to find out.

Our first full year in business was 2000, and we sold over *one million dollars*! That didn't happen by luck. We worked our asses off, stayed focused, and out-serviced all of our competition. Don't ever be afraid of competition. It makes us all rise to the occasion and be the best we can be!

## Staying Focused on Our Market

We targeted just one market, ATVs, and stayed focused on being the best at that. We didn't buy, sell, or service dirt bikes, street bikes, watercraft, or snowmobiles. Only if it were a smoking good deal would we even consider another market. It's better to narrow your focus so you know who your customers are. If everyone is your customer, no one is your customer. By staying focused and persistent, we were able to pull ahead and make a name for ourselves in the local off-road community!

We advertised the ATVs we had for sale in our local auto trader magazine. In the beginning, we started off with just one small picture ad and eventually bought an entire page. Advertising was important to our business but not as important as the business we built through word of mouth of our outstanding customer service. We brought in customers from all our surrounding states, which can mean a lot to a small business. When you are known for "something" and are good at it, people take notice and talk. That's where staying focused on just the ATV market was really helpful for us. What are you good at and what are you known for?

I recently read a book titled *Be the Best at What Matters Most*, which was written by my friend Joe

Calloway. In his book, Joe says, "If you truly are the best at what you do, are competitively priced (which may mean that you are the highest priced, as long as the value justifies it), and you are easy to do business with, you win. Every shred of evidence in the marketplace is telling us that now, more than ever, quality performance is the one sure factor that drives success."

By narrowing your market, you can more effectively reach the right customer. Since we were buying and selling just ATVs, there was no confusion about who we were marketing to.

Direct target marketing is much more effective than marketing to the masses. There is a lot of noise in today's world. People are bombarded with ads through television, radio, billboards, print, social media, and more, which make it very difficult to get your message past their tune-out filter. On average, it takes about sixteen exposures/impressions to get a customer to act on your advertising and take an interest in buying your product. By target marketing to your core audience, you can bring that number down substantially and save yourself lots of time and money.

Our dealership's success was built before the Internet and social media played such a big part in advertising and marketing. Imagine how much more we could have done if these tools had been in place. You have so much more of an advantage with technology today.

# CHAPTER 4

## Relationship Selling: The Power of People (Go Beyond Average)

Have you ever been out to eat and received bad customer service? Most people know better than to send their food back, right? That one experience will most likely determine whether you return. No matter what business you have, one of the most crucial elements to your success besides making a good quality product is providing great customer service. Still so many businesses just don't get it!

---

*Key #2: Go Beyond Average! Another key that makes us so efficient in business is that we always strive to provide a great customer experience.*

---

Our dealership's success was built on going beyond average and providing a great customer experience. We focused on going the extra mile and making our customers feel special. We included pick up and delivery of ATV's for service, we always tried to get to know each customer on a more personal level, and we made everyone feel welcome when they came into our store. We wanted to make it more than just one sale. Our goal was to make customers want to come back. I

knew if we invested in and took care of our current
dedicated customers the word of mouth from that
would pay off tenfold.

## Take Care of Existing Customers

Many businesses focus more time on advertising for
new customers when they should be focusing on
making their existing customers happy. You're just
throwing money away if you don't follow through with
good customer service. It's like a revolving door. If you
take a portion of your advertising budget and put it
into your current customers, word of mouth will travel
fast and bring you more business than you know what
to do with.

I have to share a story that is a perfect example of
what I'm talking about. We had a tour bus for our
television show that we used to travel across the
country to visit off-road parks and events. We would
always fill up at this one gas station near the office
before every road trip, which was often two times a
week. It would cost around $400 to $500 each time.
They had a coupon at the bottom of the receipt
offering a free medium coffee with fill up that we
always took advantage of. This one particular time,
the printer wasn't working at the gas pump, so
Melissa went inside to get the receipt. When she took
the medium coffee to the register, the cashier got

smart with her and told her that since she didn't have the receipt coupon from the printer at the pump, she couldn't get the free coffee.

At this point, it was no longer about the coffee but the fact that I was a loyal customer and was not being treated fairly. I went in and had a talk with the manager, who took care of the coffee and hopefully took care of the employee. Now this may seem very minor to you in your business, but this is a perfect example of how poor customer service can negatively impact your business and drive away loyal customers.

I have another perfect example from *The 7 Habits of Highly Effective People* by Stephen R. Covey. In his book, he shared a story of a restaurant that was sold and under new management but never told anyone about the change. Now this restaurant was known for their clam chowder. As a matter of fact, most days you couldn't get into the place between 11 a.m. and 2 p.m. because it was packed. Customers would take gallons of this clam chowder home with them.

The new owners were looking at ways to increase their bottom line so they decided to water down the clam chowder. The bottom line came up for the first two months, but it didn't take long for their regular customers to notice the lower-quality chowder, and sales decreased rapidly. The word got out and their business continued to slow down. The new owners tried to save the business and get it back to where it was by going back to the original recipe but their current customers had already lost faith in them and the damage was already done. If they had continued to take care of their existing customers, their business could have taken a different direction. Take care of your current dedicated customers.

## Emotion Sells Product

Just knowing someone's name or what they like to do, can make all the difference in the world. Create a direct relationship with your customers through value added marketing (VAM). By triggering someone's emotions, you can build their trust and interest in your product. If you can get to know who your customers are and then find a way to meet their needs, they will begin to understand you, like you, and even trust you, which leads to more business for you. A great example of this is how large retailers change their commercials on television during the holidays and for large events like the Super Bowl to trigger an emotion.

To be most effective in your marketing, use a familiar image or person to get through your customer's tune-out filter more quickly by providing an element of trust. That's exactly what we have done with the television show. If I tell our viewers that I use a particular product or give something a good review, they are more likely to buy that product. According to Alliance Connection Productions, 86 percent of customers engage more with a brand that creates an emotional experience. It is our job on television to build the dream of riding and the off-road lifestyle. That dream creates emotion, and the emotion is what drives our viewers to take action!

Remember, people have a choice about where they spend their money and have a tendency to put their guard up right away when they think they're being sold something. If they think you are their friend and can be trusted, they are quicker to do business with you. A good customer experience will set you apart from your competitors.

## Knowledge Is Power

By staying in the ATV market exclusively, we became very knowledgeable about the products we were selling. This further helped us develop a level of trust with our customers because we knew what we were talking about, which gave them yet another reason to buy from us. It can be very frustrating to customers when they know more about a product or service than the salesperson does.

I recently interviewed an owner of a powersports dealership and asked him what his biggest frustration in business was. His first response was finding good employees. Then he proceeded to tell me that another big frustration is when the customer expects them to know everything about the products they sell. He said they just don't have time to learn about all the products on their floor.

Knowledge is power; customers want to buy from someone who not only knows the products they're selling but also similar products sold by competitors. Knowledge and confidence will also help you handle objections and show customers the features and benefits they're looking for.

## Rapport Pays More

We didn't have a unique product because we had a few larger dealerships nearby that were selling the same things, but we did narrow down our market enough to be the best when it came to customer service and building rapport. If you have a product or service that's not unique, then it's even more important to become an expert at taking care of your customers and your relationships with them to be competitive in your marketplace. Your personality and the way you treat customers determines about 80 percent of your sales success. Look at some of the most successful businesses in the world; Chick-Fil-A, Nike, Starbucks, Fed-Ex, Red Bull, Facebook, etc. They all marketed one thing well and became known for being an expert in their field.

We had a spiral notebook behind the sales counter and took notes on each customer we talked to. Our goal was to talk to everyone that walked through our doors. We wanted to make them feel welcome and learn as much about them as we could, such as who they were, what they were looking for, what they wanted to spend, what ATVs or SXSs they already owned, their phone number, kids names, and other hobbies. Why did we do this? Rapport pays more.

No one likes being just a customer. Everyone wants to feel like you are a friend and that you care. Knowing our customers personally helped us decide what ATVs we were going to buy to sell for quick turnaround and with choosing inventory to stock of essentials like spark plugs, chains, oils, helmets, and so on.

We had a great system. I researched and bought ATVs privately and also had connections with some larger dealers a few hours away that would allow me to buy their trade-in vehicles. The spiral book with our customer notes helped us determine what ATVs I was really looking to buy. After the deal, I would call Melissa on the way back to the dealership and tell her what ATVs I had and how much I thought each was worth.

She would go through our customer list and make phone calls to people looking for that particular ATV or something similar. We sold on a first come, first serve basis, and many times we would have multiple customers at the dealership at the same time. What does everyone want? What they can't have or something everyone else wants. We would service each ATV, do the necessary repairs, and have them out the door within a day or two.

## Under Promise and Over Deliver

We also went beyond average by picking up and delivering our customer's ATVs for service and then repairing and performing regular maintenance as quickly as possible. Our shop had eight work bays, which were filled at all times. It was our goal to know what we needed for each ATV or SXS within one to two days of coming in the door and get parts ordered as quickly as possible to get our customers back out on the trail.

To customers who purchased an ATV or SXS from us, we provided a 50/50—thirty-day warranty, which included 50 percent off parts and 50 percent off labor for thirty days. We took great care of our customers and worked hard to think through each sale as if we were the customers.

We also offered special discounts on gear and accessories with every ATV or SXS purchased on the day of the sale. We put together special promotional packages at holidays and promos for kids that included a free helmet, goggles, jersey, and gloves with every kid's ATV sold.

We focused on out-servicing our competition by under promising and over delivering, and before long we had more business than we knew what to do with. It's important to add that we never compromised the market and price point. We were always competitive with our pricing but relied more on customer service, quick turn around, and great customer relationships for our success.

On one instance, I had a customer bring back his ATV within the first thirty days with a blown motor. Now, when we sold him the ATV, we told him that the oil had to be mixed with the gas for this particular unit because the injector bottle was unhooked. We also had him sign paperwork stating this. But he completely forgot to put oil in the gas and blew the engine within the first few days. He and I both knew what had happened but I still honored the 50/50 warranty and we got him back out on the trail. He was happy and brought back all of his buddies. I can't stress enough how important providing good customer service is. You make one person happy, and they tell three friends, but you make one person unhappy, and they tell twenty friends.

## Social Media in Business

With technology like Facebook, Twitter, Instagram, and others, customers are quick to voice their opinion, good or bad, to thousands of friends. And they can do that in an instant. There is so much negativity and bullying on these platforms. This is where cowards flock to post things they know nothing about to be heard by anyone who will listen. You'll find most times that the people who post negative crap are just jealous and insecure, looking to tear everyone else down because their life sucks!

It's best to take the high road on social platforms and post only good, positive information and think before you fire off a reaction to negativity. Adding fuel to the fire only gives them the satisfaction of knowing they got to you. Many times, your loyal customers will intervene and have your back. Some negative is not a bad thing on these social platforms because it shows that it's not just all biased opinions. When I notice that someone is downright rude or out of line, I just delete the post and block that individual from our social sites. If people act stupid one time, you can bet they will be stupid again.

## Hard Work Pays Off

Melissa and I both worked at the dealership from 7 a.m. to 10 p.m. every day. We basically raised our kids there, complete with a crib and playroom in the back office. Melissa took care of the Parts & Service and I was mainly in charge of buying/selling the ATVs and doing some wrenching. We also had a few mechanics working full time for us. I was still full time (60+ hours) at the printing company, so I was cutting the candle in half and burning all four ends! Our life was kind of crazy, but we were truly passionate about what we were doing and staying focused was finally paying off.

I was never afraid to work hard and that is exactly what was required with having a full-time job and a full-time business. Sometimes that meant very little sleep for me, but I kept pushing for more because I hated working at the printing company and knew it was just a matter of time before I would have to let that job go to run our family business.

After two years of working both jobs, it was time to make some changes. I had a meeting with management at the printing company where I had worked for twelve years and said, "I'm going to have to let you go." Then I gave my two-week notice and walked out a free man on my thirty-second birthday! At the time I quit the printing company, I had four weeks of vacation each year, insurance benefits for my family, and was making decent money, but it wasn't what I wanted to do with my life. I wanted more.

The day I left, the human resources manager wouldn't even shake my hand or say good-bye and told me that my well would run dry and I would be back. He assured me that I wouldn't make it. This was just another negative person trying to hold me back. Eight years later, the entire printing company shut down and everyone there was out of a job, including that manager.

## Adversity Makes You Stronger

Not long after I quit my job at the printing company, we had a customer call from another state who wanted to buy six ATVs that he planned to pick up the following day. Now this was a fairly big sale for one customer so Melissa called him and requested that he bring three different cashier's checks when he came to pick up the units and even told him how much each check should be. This single sale totaled $33,000 with all three checks.

The next day, around 7 p.m., the customer arrived with the three cashier's checks in hand, just as Melissa had requested. We completed all paperwork and as he was loading, my wife called me back into the rear office and said something was wrong because the cashier's checks were not in chronological order and she could not contact the bank to verify them because it was after 5 p.m. I immediately went out and asked the customer if we could take a picture together because he was the "customer of the month" buying so many ATVs at one time. He let me take his picture.

The next morning, we called the bank and just as we had suspected, these checks were stolen from the bank and were not valid. I can't even tell you how I felt at that moment. Out $33,000 overnight and there was nothing I could do about it. He took my ATVs to another state and sold them for drug money. The police did eventually catch up with him and he did get sentenced to prison. There was no restitution for us though because he really didn't have anything.

To top it off, our insurance company was going bankrupt and couldn't pay for any of the loss. It's times like these that really test you. Again, you need to know your "why" first, to get you through tough times like these. Our only option was to just keep on keeping on. I didn't sit around and feel sorry for myself. The entire experience was a good lesson for us and we became stronger and smarter as a result.

We continually grow and learn each day on this trail with patches of gravel and roadblocks put in our paths to make us stronger. If we didn't have challenges, we wouldn't grow. It's not what happens to you, it's how you handle what happens to you. Take each situation and learn something from it.

## Our Next Big Adventure

As our business kept growing year after year, life was getting a little easier, but we were still trading time for money because we put in a lot of hours at the dealership. It was nothing to have sales reaching $30,000 to $40,000 every weekend. With growth, we were consistently busy leaving little time for us to be doing what our customers were doing, which was enjoying family time out on the trail. This led me to my next adventure—starting a TV show. There was really only one obstacle, convincing Melissa we should do this. Now keep in mind that I had NO experience doing anything like this so I had my work cut out for me!

I used to watch Bill Jordan's *Realtree Outdoors* hunting show every weekend and thought it would be pretty cool to do something like that. I can still remember approaching Melissa at the dealership with the idea to start our own off-road television show. She thought I was crazy.

I went out and bought two BIG shoulder-mount cameras, you know the old cameras that weighed 50 pounds, and brought them back to the ATV store. Melissa immediately looked at me and said, "You take those back right now. I know they cost a lot of money." She was NOT happy with me but I was persistent.

I didn't have any experience in television, being a host or even video production so this was a whole new direction, but I was willing to learn. It was still the same industry though so I'm still staying focused, or at least that's what I was trying to sell my wife on.

I was determined to make this work, but Melissa was leery of the idea because we were pretty comfortable financially with the dealership and already working a ton of hours. She just couldn't imagine having any extra time to do something more. As a matter of fact, the dealership kept us so busy that our time was controlling us. We were like a hamster running on a wheel from one day to the next. It's important to keep yourself busy but stay productive, always working toward a goal. My new goal was to regain more quality time with my family.

There is a real difference between staying busy and being productive. Being busy comes from not knowing what the target or goal is for the day which is a direct result of not making a "to do" list and prioritizing every day.

How do you know if you're being productive? At the end of the day, did you accomplish anything, make progress or get results to get you closer to your goal? Being productive is when you know exactly what your target or goal is for the day and do the most important task first until it is completed then move on to complete the second highest priority task on your list and so on. Being productive takes discipline but has far greater rewards than just keeping yourself busy.

# CHAPTER 5

## The Power of Persistence: I'll Figure It Out (Persistence, Fear, & Failure)

What would you do if you knew you couldn't fail? Would you set your goals a little higher? Would you take more chances? Fear and failure go hand in hand. There are many different kinds of FEAR: fear of doing something, fear of rejection or the word "NO," fear of failure, fear of being broke, fear of success (what if you do become successful, how will your life change?), and so on. Your desire, goals, and dreams need to be clear and detailed or else the first time you come face to face with fear or rejection, you'll give up and shut down. Here's a quote by hockey icon Wayne Gretzky that is worth thinking deeply about, "You will miss 100 percent of the shots you don't take." Imagine the possibilities if you took more chances.

For me, the fear of failure and not having the means to take care of my family was enough to make me do whatever it took to be successful. I'm not talking about failure as in I tried something and it didn't work. I'm talking about totally giving up on myself and not pushing harder to succeed. In the past, we have been so broke and in debt that we couldn't even afford a gallon of milk, let alone pay our rent for our apartment, which was only $350 a month and included utilities. At one point, I owed the IRS over $80,000 in back taxes and was ready to go to jail. That all scared the hell out of me and I NEVER want to go back! That's why I work so hard to keep moving forward and stretch myself to do the next uncomfortable thing. I want to progress in life and be able to give back. There is no feeling in this world like having a purpose and being able to help someone in need.

## Keep Getting Back Up

It's important to keep in mind that everyone makes mistakes. That's just life. You can't dwell on the mistakes you've made. Think of these as lessons in life, stepping stones, if you will. Put them on a shelf and move on. I've made a lot of mistakes but have learned from each and every one of them. Winners pick themselves up and move on. It's when you stay down that you don't win. Don't EVER give up on yourself. You were put here for a reason. What is that reason?

---

*Key #3: Be Persistent! Another important key that helped us get to where we are is powering through challenges with persistence.*

---

It's a given that in life and in business you're going to come up against setbacks and hardships, it's just a part of the turf. We've been dealing with this through every business venture that we've taken on and at this point in the game, nothing surprises me. I appreciate my successes because of my failures, if that makes sense. When you fall down but get back up to keep fighting, you succeed and win. Those lessons are hands on, the real deal and when you're faced with a particular challenge again, you'll know exactly what to do.

## Proven Time and Time Again

My favorite stories of failure and persistence feature Colonel Sanders and Walt Disney. Did you know that Harland David Sanders aka Colonel Sanders worked and lost dozens of jobs before founding his successful ' restaurant chain, Kentucky Fried Chicken? He was sixty-five years old, retired, and had received his first social security check for $99 when he decided to take his "finger lickin' good" chicken recipe door to door to local businesses and restaurants to promote and sell it. He went through 1,009 "No's" before he got his first "Yes."

Walt Disney's was another great story of perseverance and courage in failure. He went through bankruptcy several times starting at age twenty-two while in pursuit of his dream. A newspaper editor fired Walt Disney and accused him of being lazy, lacking imagination, having no good ideas. In his own words, Walt Disney said, "All the adversity I've had in my life, all my troubles and obstacles, have strengthened me . . . You may not realize it when it happens, but a kick in the teeth may be the best thing in the world for you."

Thomas Edison's teachers told him he was "too stupid to learn anything." He went on to hold more than 1,000 patents and invented some world-changing devices, like the phonograph, practical electrical lamp, and a movie camera.

Henry Ford's early businesses failed and left him broke five times before he founded the successful Ford Motor Company.

Steven Spielberg was rejected by the University of Southern California School of Cinematic Arts multiple times.

J.K. Rowling was a single mom living off welfare when she began writing the first *Harry Potter* novel. She eventually became the first billionaire author in 2004.

Theodor Seuss Geisel, better known as Dr. Seuss, had his first book rejected by twenty-seven different publishers.

While developing his vacuum, Sir James Dyson went through 5,126 failed prototypes and his savings over fifteen years. But the 5,127th prototype worked and the Dyson brand became the best-selling bagless vacuum in the United States. He is now worth an estimated $4.5 billion according to *Forbes*.

## How Badly Do You Want It?

According to the Small Business Administration (SBA), 30 percent of new businesses fail within the first year, 50 percent of new businesses fail within the first five years, and 66 percent of new businesses fail within the first ten years. The odds are not stacked in your favor, but it is up to you to fall on the winning side.

Looking back, I know persistence played a huge part in our dealership being successful. Everything from finding the resources for the finances to start the dealership, to making the far-flung trips to buy the ATVs, and then working long, hard hours to keep the sales moving involved persistence. We were not afraid to work hard.

That first year of trying to get our TV show off the ground was probably the most challenging thing I've ever done. Between trying to figure out cameras and networks, to learning how to host and doing a pilot show, to obtaining sponsors and press, you could say I had my hands full. The hardest part was that I was pretty much doing everything on my own because I had to prove myself to Melissa because she was not yet on board with my crazy idea.

The most defining moment of my life was probably when we went to the annual dealer trade show for our industry and I was going around to different booths telling everyone we were going to have a television show. What I was doing was looking for free press and sponsorships. At that time, we really didn't have anything, but as we were walking around the trade show I kept giving my pitch, "Hey I'm Brian Fisher and I'm starting a new television show."

Melissa was so mad at me. She told me to stop telling everyone we were going to have a television show. I would wait until she walked away and hit everyone up anyway. One booth we went up to was one of the largest magazines in the off-road industry, and I happened to come face to face with the publisher there. I told him my name and what I was planning to do, and he straight up laughed in my face. I'm not talking a little chuckle. He was full blown, doubled over with laughter. He then proceeded to tell me that I had no talent, no acting experience, no money, just nothing to make this happen! He told me that I was wasting his time. I told him, "You don't understand. I *will* have a TV show."

As Melissa and I turned and started walking away, I could almost feel her glaring eyes burning the side of my head. I didn't want to look at her until we got far enough away from that bunghole. We hadn't even gotten five steps when Melissa looked at me and said, "Oh, we *will* have a TV show!" That was the defining moment that I needed because from that day forward she was 100 percent on board and helped me with my dream of pulling off the show.

At the time, I didn't know that this magazine was producing their own television show to be launched and that the publisher was slated to be the host. So ultimately, there were ulterior motives behind his criticisms. Jumping ahead, they did get their ATV show up and running, but it was short lived. He eventually called me years later for a favor and apologized for our initial meeting and congratulated us on our accomplishments.

## Losing Is Not an Option

We built our success on the foundation of my vision. What you see, you will believe. I could see us having a television show long before Melissa could see it, and I didn't give up on convincing her that I could do it.

What you see is what will be. Think about this, if race car drivers have a fear of hitting the wall and that's all they focus on during the race, you can bet at some point in time, they will end up hitting the wall. That's exactly why you need to focus on your "why" or your "destination" and keep moving in that direction. Stay away from negative thoughts that will do nothing but hold you back and send you off course.

As I pursued the television show idea, I knew it wasn't going to be easy, but I didn't realize how much of a challenge it would be. I was committed to making fifteen to thirty phone calls a day, Monday through Friday to look for sponsors, which is what we needed to get things up and running. Now this was on top of helping run the dealership. I needed to prove to Melissa that I could do this. You might be thinking fifteen to thirty phone calls a day is a lot, but it's really not when you're getting hung up on and leaving lots of messages. I found out real quick that just because you have cameras doesn't mean you have a television show.

I got my ass handed to me the first few months because I didn't have a clue what I was doing. It was like throwing me into a shark tank dealing with larger companies, ad agencies, and networks. I was hung up on and cussed at. You name it; it happened, but giving up was not an option. Melissa's office and mine were beside each other in the dealership and she could hear some of my crazy phone calls and would just laugh, thinking this is never going to work.

I stayed focused because I knew if I slung enough mud, something would stick. Making sales is just a numbers game. Most sales are made after eight contacts, but many people give up after three to four attempts. You have to go through a lot of "No's" in order to get a "Yes." Every time I got a "No," I was one step closer to a "Yes." One year later I got my first YES from Yamaha, and I acted just like it had happened twenty other times. My persistence was paying off. It was really rewarding to see my plan coming together!

## Doing Your Homework

I soon got smart and started using the same concept that had made our dealership so successful— providing a great customer experience. Remember Rapport pays more? These agencies and companies that I had been calling on for sponsorship were just people. So I started writing down little notes about specific things they told me (personal things like a vacation, birthday, and so on), and I would bring the conversation back to them and show an interest. I also researched the companies I was contacting and got to know their product before I called, which allowed me to give them real-world ideas on how I could incorporate their product into our show. Having them picture what I was seeing was key. They were busy working on their business and loved being presented with creative ideas to market their products. It was no longer about them just buying what I was selling and giving me money to fuel my dreams. I made each phone call about them and how I could help them. If you help enough people get what they want, you'll get what you want.

I went after the biggest and the best companies in the off-road industry to sponsor our television show because I knew it would be good for their business, for our business, and for our show. If you sell out to just anyone, your name is no longer worth anything and customers will lose trust in you and your standards. Believe me; I have already turned down a six-figure check because I did not have faith in a company.

I called on one particular company, Rick's Motorsport Electrics, a few times a week as we were trying to get our television show started. The owner's wife would take my calls and after talking with her for months on end, she finally asked her husband "Would you at least give this guy a chance and talk to him?" The reason for my persistence with them was because we sold their products in our ATV dealership and I knew they were the best at what they did.

The first time I talked to Rick Shaw we hit it off right away. That was in 2001 and Rick and Donna Shaw have become not only great partners of our show but also some of our best friends. We go to the Virgin Islands with them every year to catch up, vacation, and have a great time. My rule of thumb when calling on potential partners is to keep calling back until I get a flat out "No." This is another great example of being persistent and not being afraid to fail.

## First Things First

An important key to persistence is to do the most difficult thing on your list *first* every day. At that time for me, it was making the sales phone calls. I knew that procrastination was only wasting my time and energy, which made me less productive the rest of the day. If I had a phone call or meeting that I was dreading, I would take care of it first thing in the morning. If you let these kinds of things go, they will take over your whole day and make you miserable, leaving you with very little productivity.

Now speaking of productivity, I found something very interesting when listening to the *Insane Productivity* course by Darren Hardy, publisher of *Success* magazine: Studies show that when you multitask, your IQ drops ten points, creates stress, you are less efficient, and you are actually giving yourself "self-induced" or "acquired ADD." When you think you're multitasking, you're actually just switching back and forth from one task to another meaning you never get one thing done to your full potential. It's better to commit to one task at a time and focus on the top three things and get them done instead of trying to get ten things done halfway. To get the most productivity, it is important to get your highest priority task off your plate first thing in the morning so you can clear your mind for the rest of the day.

## The Focus Formula to Persist

1. Make your "To Do" list every day.
2. Make #1 the most important thing on your list and then follow with #2, etc.
3. Always do the highest priority task first or you'll be stressed out about it all day.
4. Stick to only doing the project you're working on. Do NOT skip around or move to the next one until the task you're working on is complete.

5. Put your phone away or in airplane mode. One little text, call, or interruption from a friend or colleague can totally change your focus.
6. Your goal here is to do each task to its fullest potential and be productive, not just busy. The world is full of busy multitasking unproductive people. Once you master the skill of "focus," persistence will follow.

## Don't Underestimate Me

Another company I was trying to get a partnership with was Honda. I knew they were one of the top ATV companies and getting through to the right person was a challenge in itself. I called their ad agency and got my ass handed to me several times but kept going back looking for another way to get my foot in the door.

After many phone calls to Honda directly, someone finally took my phone call from the ATV Product Management Team. He didn't give me the time of day but did answer my call so now I had a name and contact there. I called him about every other week until I finally got his attention.

He asked me what I was going to do different than the other ATV television shows and I told him that I was just going to "keep it real," build the dream, and showcase the lifestyle of ATV riding. He paused for a little and I thought he had hung up, but my response had finally gotten his attention and he said, "Tell me more."

After a brief conversation, he told me that if I was serious, I should come to Las Vegas the next day for a new ATV introduction they were having. I got off the phone, immediately bought our plane tickets, and the very next day, we were in the Grand Canyon with Honda. He was very surprised to see us. When I got out of the taxi van, he asked me who I was and I introduced myself. He said, "I can't believe you came. Do you know how many people I tell that to and they never show up?" That was just the beginning of our adventures in proving ourselves to this industry.

## Going Above and Beyond

In the beginning, we drove to personally meet many of our potential sponsors, but at the time we really didn't have the extra money for hotels and gas so we slept in our truck. That was how we were going beyond average, doing what most people would not be willing to do. With the technology of today, most business communication happens via phone calls and emails, but there is nothing like a good, sit-down, face-to-face meeting. Another way to set yourself apart is to mail a handwritten thank-you card after your meeting. This will show you're serious and provide an element of trust.

## Paying the Price to Win

Sometimes things don't work in your favor though, like the time we drove to Minnesota for an appointment to meet an agency that represented a potential sponsor. Now keep in mind that this was in the very beginning when we really didn't have the funds to do much traveling. After a twelve-hour drive, we finally arrived. The receptionist called up to the person we were supposed to meet, and I could hear her on the other end of the line saying, "Tell them to leave their materials with you. I'm busy and don't have time to see them."

Now the receptionist knew that I had just heard what had been said, and she didn't know how to react. I jokingly, but seriously said, "Which car is hers?" I was furious. The thought even crossed my mind to break every one of her car windows and make her tires flat. It was not fun being in that moment, but looking back, that was just another "No" that led us to a "Yes." The funny thing is, a few years later we met a new marketing manager for this same company and ended up closing a deal just shy of $300,000. This is a perfect example of why you should never burn bridges because you never know where the road might lead.

I also had one meeting where an employee of another company I was working with told me I wasn't worth the money I was asking. Actually, this was a very small partnership, and not long after our meeting, that employee was let go from his position. I guess he wasn't worth the money he was asking as well. It's funny how things work out.

## Caution: Bumpy Road Ahead

Our first year on television, we self-funded our show so we could be on the air. This cost us approximately $250,000—getting our pilot done two times (the first time we were ripped off because we didn't know what we were doing); hiring a full time editor (which didn't pan out the way we thought it would); network airtime (even more expensive than we anticipated); plus the costs of cameras and all of the equipment, a music license, multiple kinds of insurance; and all the travel for the show. Fortunately, our ATV dealership was doing well and we were able to take some funds from there to put into the television idea.

During our first few years in television, it was a real challenge to keep our heads above water as we entered into an agreement to sell our dealership with a three-year balloon payment in the contract terms. Three years is a long time to wait to get paid for a sale. Melissa and I took a HUGE pay cut so that we could maintain our business bills and pay our team of people. We slept in our truck many times as we traveled, visiting potential sponsors to build relationships. We made less than any of our staff for years but stayed focused on the bigger picture and where we were going.

Several times our office administrator came to me on Wednesday and told me she needed $15,000 or $20,000 by Friday for accounts payable. I would always say "I'll figure it out" and I would. We lived paycheck to paycheck in business for the first couple years but we got through it.

Finding finances or having difficulty with finances seems to be one of the biggest struggles for many small businesses. We know because we have been there. Getting money to start your business will be one of the most difficult things you need to do. Keep in mind that it's just a numbers game. Walt Disney was turned down 302 times before he found a bank to believe in his dream. You need to learn from every "No" and refine your pitch and business plan to be more in line with what potential lenders might be looking for. You can make a good start by doing your research on the bank before your meeting to pitch your idea.

I obviously didn't comprehend this at first because after we got shot down by every traditional bank in our local area, our initial funding to start our ATV dealership came in the form of $5,000 loan at 28 percent interest from a high-interest rate loan company. We had to start somewhere in building the foundation of our financial relationships. Start small and stay on top of your financial obligations by putting it as your first priority. Eventually, your credit score and line of credit will continue to increase, which will give you more choices down the road.

As we continued to build our credit, we met with a local traditional bank again to review our options for freeing up some cash to help build our business and invest in the television show. We finally got the ball rolling with the branch manager and business lending division at this particular bank and started with a small loan and built on that. Over the years, we developed a great relationship at this bank with many business loans to follow. It's very important for every business to maintain a great banking relationship.

Not long after our move to Tennessee, we met with that branch manager for lunch while on a business trip to Pennsylvania and recalled our initial bank meetings. She told us that she had been willing to give us a loan because when we failed we kept getting back up and pushing forward. She said she preferred to give loans to people with a few bumps in their past rather than someone who never faced any challenges or adversity. Her thought was that the first time the person with a perfect record comes up against hardships or big problems; they will be more likely to give up rather than push through it.

Another option for short-term financing is to solicit help from your family or friends. There were a few times when finding finances required us to reach out to my dad and mom for help in the form of a short-term loan but I always did what I said I was going to do and paid back every penny. My family has always been there for me because they watched me fail over and over again but never give up. Truthfully, the tougher things got, the harder I tried. Giving up was just not an option for me. My brother Scott and his wife Christa also came to our rescue when we were in the early stages of selling our dealership and transitioning to the television show. They saw the commitment we were making to the dealership and the TV show and helped us out of a bind by loaning us money when we needed help most. Always remember, when people step up and loan you money, paying them back is top priority, even if it requires you to set up monthly payments. That builds your integrity and keeps the lines of communication open.

Bumpy roads are not always about finding finances. Sometimes it can be a road that takes you completely out of your comfort zone. I didn't have any experience being in front of the camera or even running a camera for that matter but I wasn't going to let fear stop me. As I mentioned earlier, I was a total introvert all my life, so getting in front of a video camera and going back to review the footage took some getting used to. It wasn't my idea of a dream job. We are always more critical of ourselves than others are of us, so this was a personal challenge that I had to overcome. I did it by reminding myself that being uncomfortable was key in moving forward and I always kept my eye on the prize—my "why."

Another big issue we were faced with, in the first few years of being on the air, was being kicked off the Outdoor Channel in the middle of our contract. This meant we could not fulfill all of our partnership agreements. Our show wasn't the only show to be kicked off the air. The program director at the time didn't see eye to eye with us and a few other producers and we lost $250,000 in sponsorship dollars in two weeks. We did eventually find another network for a temporary home, so we were able to fulfill the rest of our sponsorship agreements.

One year later, the new network we were on went bankrupt, which was no real surprise. I recall being on a shoot with a large sponsor in West Virginia when I got the call. Fortunately, I had already been in discussions with the new programming director at Outdoor Channel and had our show picked back up. It just took some strategic planning and always looking three to four moves ahead with our business in order to stay on top of all of this. You should always think six months out on every move you make and how it will affect your business. This strategy kept our heads above water many times in our businesses.

## There Will Be Detours

In September 2008, we saw the writing on the wall for the future of the powersports business. Our sponsorships were dropping and cutting back due to the economy. ATV sales would drop over 65 percent in the next couple years. We had to shift gears but still stay in our lane and stay focused. We had to adapt to the change in our industry so we started to put more attention on riding parks, events, and aftermarket accessories rather than relying on the manufacturers for sponsorship dollars.

People were still riding and fixing their ATVs but not buying new units. We also looked outside the powersports industry in markets like tires, oil, insurance, locks, and so on. Don't be afraid to try new things and think along new lines. Adapt with changes and technology, for example, use social media or other platforms like cell phones for advertising.

If the music industry hadn't adapted to downloads and had relied solely on direct CD sales, imagine where they would be. It's important to stay one step ahead and think outside the box. If we hadn't done this, my television career would have been over. There's change in every business and you need to adapt and power through these roadblocks to keep moving forward. Giving up is not an option.

In 2010, we were still focused heavily on going after off-road parks and riding areas, so I presented our staff with an idea of getting a tour bus and wrapping it with sponsors who would pay to have their logo on the wrap. Then we could also charge the off-road parks for each visit. They thought I was crazy and said it wouldn't work.

I stayed focused on this business plan and it all came together in 2011. On our first year of the tour, we pulled together enough sponsors to pay off the tour bus and have extra cash for the wrap, fuel, maintenance, and so on. The next two years, were profitable and when we sold the tour bus four years later, it was all profit. If I had listened to everyone in the office, none of this would have happened.

Life is full of obstacles. If you don't fight, you won't win! There will always be situations that you come up against, but having a winning attitude means finding a way to get over it, go through it, around it, under it, or whatever it takes to get you to the next obstacle. If your GPS says "Roadblock Ahead," you don't stop heading toward your destination. That's when you reroute to find a different road and keep going. This same principle applies to life. There are several routes to your destination, but you need to find the road that's right for you.

## Go The Extra Mile

We wanted to be the BEST at the television show, so we would outwork everyone else. Our partners recognized all the hard work and passion we put into this. We used the same concept of under promise and over deliver with our partners, always going the extra mile and treating them and their products like they were our own business. Put yourself in their shoes and ask yourself, "What would I want if I were the customer buying this product or service?" That will help keep you on the right track.

Whether I was dealing with a customer at the dealership or a corporate partner for the television show, I always asked what I could do for them and then I listened. Some people would tell me exactly what they wanted, but many times I had to offer advice or give creative input to help them picture what I was seeing. I've even provided a "freebie" or great deal to corporate companies by producing a product profile or product placement inside the show just to get my foot in the door, which led to sponsorship dollars down the road many times. This really depended on who I was dealing with and how much I wanted them to be a part of what we had going on.

It all comes down to hunger. How badly do you want it? No matter how big or small the obstacle, having a "do whatever it takes" attitude is key. Don't be afraid to take risks. I was never a gambler on other things, but when it comes to myself, I would risk it all.

# CHAPTER 6

## Defining Moments on Your Road to Success

We all have those unforgettable moments in life that I refer to as *defining moments*. Those are the stories you never forget because they've made an impact on your life in some sort of way, good or bad. Three of my most defining moments that hit me hard I mentioned earlier: Melissa leaving and taking everything; not being able to buy my son a 35¢ pretzel; and then the publisher laughing in my face, which made Melissa get on board with the television show. There is no doubt that my life has been full of defining moments but there are a few others that I recall that I would like to share along with the lessons I learned from them.

### The Penny Story

Earlier I mentioned that Melissa and I were involved in an MLM business and really didn't have the money for travel. My main transportation at that time was this big old white, heavy Chevy van with windows that made it look like a mini school bus. My parents sold it to us for next to nothing because we didn't have a vehicle at the time. This van was a major gas hog! I think it got about five miles to the gallon.

One night I was out late working our MLM business when the van ran out of gas. I drifted into a gas station and had no money in my wallet for gas. I looked in the ashtray and counted 161 pennies, so I put $1.61 worth of gas in my van. I took the ashtray into the store and dumped it on the counter. Now I don't know if someone was playing a sick joke on me or what but one penny was stuck to the bottom of the ashtray and I couldn't get it out. I asked the cashier if she had a screwdriver or something sharp to get that last penny. She was so mad. She just pointed to the door and said "OUT." I'm pretty sure that's where the whole penny idea "Need One, Take One; Have One, Leave One" came from.

This lack of gas money experience made me realize that I did not want to live my life without money. That's when the burning desire to have a $5 bill in my pocket and a full tank of gas pushed me harder to get out of my comfort zone.

## Car Trouble

For years, Melissa and I drove nothing but junk and pushed more vehicles and walked more than we cared to. When my wife was eight months pregnant with our third child, we were en route for her ultrasound appointment when my 1970 banana yellow Chevy Blazer decided to die in the middle of an intersection with no one around. Needless to say, our only option was to have Melissa help me push it off to the side of the road until we could get it started. When we finally arrived at the appointment, the doctor couldn't figure out why our baby's heart was beating so fast. It probably wasn't the best idea to have her help me push the Chevy, but we got it done.

A few weeks later, Melissa went into labor, which lasted about twenty-four hours. The hospital gave her a pill to help her relax and sent us home giving her more time to dilate. While Melissa was sleeping, someone stopped by our house to buy the Chevy. Now keep in mind, this was our one and only means of transport, but we really needed the money and he had cash in hand. I sold the Blazer and then had to frantically find a vehicle that I could borrow to take her back to the hospital for delivery. I pulled it off while she was sleeping, but it definitely was not my best idea. Fortunately for both of us, it panned out.

We've both always had a "do whatever it takes" attitude and this was yet another great example of the tenacity of our team.

## Kids and Dog Dilemmas

When we were just getting our dealership going, I scraped together all the extra cash we had to buy a Yamaha PW50 motorcycle. I bought it brand new from a dealer at a great deal so we could resell it to make a good profit. I came home from my printing job to find that my four- and five-year-old kids had spray painted the entire bike black.

Needless to say, I was not happy. Not long after that, I got another great deal on a Suzuki DS80 dirt bike, and I looked out the window and saw our yellow lab puppy tearing the seat apart and dragging it around in our driveway. I called to get another seat and it was on back order for six months. These types of occurrences made me think real long and hard about opening a dealership! I seriously thought maybe this isn't my calling.

Challenges may come your way but they don't last forever. It's just a temporary situation, and you should always remind yourself that things could always be worse. Fix it and move on.

### I Need to Pay Uncle Sam?

When we started the television show and sold our dealership, we didn't have the incoming cash flow we'd had when we had both businesses going. We sold the dealership on a sales-lease agreement, and we took monthly payments of $1,500 for three years. This was a huge cut in income. During the first couple years we were on the air, we only had a few sponsors, so eventually something had to give.

We had a few people on our staff and decided it was more important to pay them and pay for our airtime rather than paying taxes to Uncle Sam. I didn't think the IRS would miss it and figured I would be able to get caught up before they came knocking. I was wrong!

I can still remember it like it was yesterday. We received a call from our accountant on a Wednesday morning, and he said he needed Melissa and me to stop by his office to see him because he had something to go over with us. Now you need to understand that we have the most laid back, soft-spoken accountant you would ever meet. I can still remember him telling me, "Now Brian, if you don't come up with $80,000 in two weeks, you're going to jail." I said, "Excuse me, Myke, but it sounded like you just said I was going to jail?" That didn't fit into my business plan.

We went back to our office and I immediately started packing my bags for the first flight out of town. No, I'm just kidding. That's certainly what I felt like doing. Instead, I got on the phone and started dialing for dollars and closed a two-year television sponsorship deal for $85,000. This was half of what we normally sold it for, but we had the check for the full $80,000 in our accountant's hand by Friday, which saved me from going to jail. Sometimes you have to make sacrifices to get past the tough spots. In this instance, I had learned a costly lesson the hard way.

It is amazing what you can do when your back is against the wall. Some of our best deals were done under pressure when we knew we needed to make it happen. Most great victories are won in the last few moments. Would you give up if you were in a situation like this or would you keep fighting to win? That's what defines you.

## Stranded in Mexico

Another dirt road memory that I would definitely put in the category of a defining moment came when we went on an ATV trip to Copper Canyon in Mexico. This was a guided trip with a tour company that we had used before. Unfortunately, what we didn't know was that this guide was going through a really dark period in his life. His wife was along on the trip when all hell broke loose and we found ourselves stuck in the middle.

Our guide's wife came along with us and our camera crew all day to do some bass fishing on a lake. When we returned, our guide was beyond drunk. He bragged to our camera guys that he had hooked up with one of the maids at the lodge where we were staying. Then he made his wife sit out in the hallway while we all had dinner. It was a very uncomfortable situation.

The next morning, we met up to head to the next lodge, which was a full day's ride away and he was a complete ass. We drove our side by sides about seven hours that day with no food or water. When we finally arrived, I asked him what the plan was and he told me we were on our own. He said Paco (his Mexican friend who didn't speak any English) would take us to the train station the next morning.

When we booked this trip, the guide had specifically told us not to bring any cash because we could be robbed, and we had followed his direction. I should also point out that none of us could speak Spanish so we had no idea what was in store for us. That night was uneasy to say the least. We were in a vulnerable situation in unfamiliar territory, eight hours from the US border with no food, no water, no money, and a lunatic guide who was very unpredictable.

The next morning, we loaded our bags in the back of Paco's pickup truck and he drove us to a train station in the middle of nowhere. We had no way to communicate with Paco and we couldn't read any of the Spanish signs or speak to anyone. We waited for six hours before a train showed up. We were eight hours deep into Copper Canyon so this was going to be a long train ride.

As the train came into the station, we held up our credit cards and asked if they took credit and before we knew it, they had our bags thrown onto the train and we were seated. The next thing that happened was like something straight out of a movie. A guy came through saying "Ticket, Ticket" in very broken English. But we didn't have any tickets. He said without hesitation "I'll be back."

Then suddenly a bunch of young men with assault rifles pointed at our heads were surrounding us. They said they were going to stop the train and throw us out in the middle of the canyon. We begged and pleaded and told them we would get them the money when we got to our destination—Chihuahua—which was eight hours away. The cost of our train ride immediately went up an additional $500.

Once we arrived in Chihuahua, they separated us into two groups, holding me hostage along with one of my cameramen until they got the money. Another cameraman and Melissa were taken to an ATM machine down a dark alley to retrieve the money. And of course, now each of these guys required an additional $50 tip for taking them to the ATM. They got their money and we booked a plane back to the US the next day, but that trip cost us an additional $3,000 and tested our ability to remain calm under extreme stress. If we hadn't had that money, what would have happened? Safe to say, there will be no more trips booked to Mexico with that guide.

This experience required us to work together as a team and think ahead so we could get out of there safely. We quickly learned that you shouldn't trust everyone and need to be prepared to take on unexpected challenges when they come your way. Staying focused on the ultimate goal of our safety and survival was key.

## The Costa Rica Jungle Challenge

We've had lots of adventures around the country and around the world. Some have become defining moments on our journey because of the special friendships we built and the lessons we learned along the way. That holds true for our adventure when we took on the Costa Rica Jungle Challenge to film two television episodes. This was a ten-day adventure through the Costa Rican Jungle on an ATV, which offered lots of challenges and technical riding. We took our friend Jim, who worked with *Dirt Wheels* magazine, along with us on this trip. He was there to do a story on us doing the Jungle Challenge.

On this trip, we met some truly great people, learned about trust and even more about working as a team when we came face to face with real adversity. Everyone spoke Spanish, except us. Our guide, Manrique, was the only Costa Rican that also spoke English so he acted as a translator many times on this trip. Everyone we met there was so nice and would give you their last piece of bread if it came right down to it. I say that because this really did happen when we got stuck in a monsoon.

We were about five days into our Jungle Challenge and we had come up against some pretty gnarly trails already. I'm talking trails that had you sideways and riding on the side of your machine because your handlebar was touching the ground. Costa Rica is a rain forest so we always had rain. This makes the trails and roads difficult because it causes washouts where parts of the road just wash down the side of the mountain. That day we had been riding our ATVs all day because rain had made the rivers too high to cross and we'd had to find a new route.

Now picture this, it's about 3 a.m. and you're in the middle of the jungle in Costa Rica with no civilization for miles. It is so dark that you can't see anything more than two feet in front of you. All you hear is the rushing river and monkeys howling from the tree canopy above. We were in a hurry because we were all tired and wanted to get to a place where we could rest. I was riding as close to the leader as possible so I could follow his taillights and path because I never knew when the trail would just fall off due to a washout.

All of the sudden, I hear one of my cameramen in a panic on the two-way radio yelling "Brian, Jim! Hurry! It's bad!" I turned around and headed back to see what had happened. When I got there, I saw Jim lying lifeless on the ground. His helmet was cracked and his shirt ripped off his back. His skin looked gray. I thought he was dead.

Jim had been traveling pretty fast when he'd hit a washout, which sent him tumbling down the mountain, flipping his ATV several times. His collarbone was broken and protruding about three inches from his neck. Fortunately, the bone didn't come through his skin or he could have bled to death right there in front of us. Jim was unconscious and our guide Manrique was freaking out.

After several minutes, we finally got Jim alert but he was in shock and in so much pain that he was delusional. We were miles from civilization and still had a few rivers to cross in the complete darkness. Melissa was on the back of my Can Am Two-Up ATV so I had her drive his ATV (which was pretty messed up) and put him on the back with me.

It was a matter of life or death to get Jim out of the jungle and to a medic. However, the rushing river we needed to cross was about seventy feet wide and running so swiftly that it could sweep us downstream in a heartbeat in the total darkness. I was confident I could ride my ATV across the river with my friend Jim on the back to get him to safety. My concern for his health was far greater than my fear of what might happen to me.

Manrique was arguing with me saying, "No Señor Fisher, you will die if you try and take him across." Our guide was still in shock so I had to assure him, "No Manrique. I can do it. I know it in my heart. I've done it before!" With Jim on the back, I pointed the ATV upstream against the current and drove in at an angle so that it could carry me to the riverbank on the other side as I floated downstream. This river was deep. As I entered, I kept on the gas, and the headlights on my ATV were completely submerged. My Can Am ATV was more like a jet ski, but I knew that if I kept on the gas and didn't let water back into the tailpipe, it would keep going. Everyone started cheering as I got to the other side.

Now I had to somehow get back across this raging river to get the rest of the ATVs. As I was standing on the edge of the river I heard, "*Dame tu mano.*" I could barely hear it over the noise of the river, and then I heard it again, "*Dame tu mano.*" I had no idea what it meant. It could have meant anything but I went on faith.

As I started walking into the river, my knee-high rubber boots filled up right away making them ten times heavier and harder to walk in. Then I saw one of Manrique's friends standing in the river. He had his hand out saying, "*Dame tu mano.*" I don't speak Spanish but then it hit me. He was saying, "Give me your hand." As I reached out to his hand, he grabbed mine and passed me along to the next guy. They made a human chain across the river. No one felt confident enough to drive their ATVs over by themselves, so I did this eight times until we had all the ATVs across.

We did eventually get out of the jungle and got Jim to a witch doctor, which was an adventure all its own. If all of us had not worked together as a team that night, trusting one another and being persistent, this story could have easily ended differently. Just as Jim lost control coming off that mountain, your trail might lead you off course, but having a "do whatever it takes" attitude can get you through it. This is a great example of staring fear in the face and overcoming all obstacles.

## Sweet Revenge

My story of sweet revenge is another defining moment for my family and me. You see, when we had our ATV dealership, we bought the house directly across the street from the dealership, which is where we lived and raised our family for the next ten years. We had this one absolutely miserable neighbor, as everyone does, that no one could stand. She hated life and everyone around her and would do whatever she could to make you mad.

On several occasions, our kids would be down in the woods behind our house playing and she would get her shotgun out and shoot into the woods. She also yelled at them and Melissa several times about her property line and what she expected. There was talk that she even poisoned neighborhood pets that ventured her way. She and her husband would do everything they could to try to put a damper on our businesses and dreams. Her theory was that she had lived in the neighborhood first so she was in charge. A few times she called the township to complain about the dealership noise. If we were filming behind our house, she would fire up her tractor or the weed trimmer and run it just to create an annoyance. If you looked in the dictionary for a neighbor from hell, her face would be there. She had it out for me.

I never left her get to me and always stayed focused on where we were going. As we were getting the "Keepin' It Real Tour" together and making plans for the wrap on the tour bus, I knew just what I wanted to do. We wrapped the entire tour bus with a riding scene and put a picture of me on the side—both sides about ten feet tall—and parked it right at the top of our driveway where she had to look at my face for the next three years, every single day.

The fourth year of our tour was bittersweet as we made the move to Tennessee, thirteen hours away, and left behind our wretched neighbor who will continue her life of unhappiness and despair in that small town that she thinks she runs.

Sometimes having an enemy or nemesis is a blessing in disguise because it makes you push harder and become stronger to see things through. Frank Sinatra said, "The best revenge is massive success," which I couldn't agree with more.

## The End of the Line

Another defining moment happened when my father (who was actually my grandfather) was hospitalized on the tail end of pneumonia and suffering a bad urinary tract infection. Hospice came in to take care of him. They told me he was very weak and was not getting any better; they expected him to pass away by Monday. Now this was on a Thursday and I was scheduled to go on a really important video shoot ten hours away that weekend. I was all over the place in my head on this one. Should I stay or should I go? I talked to my dad and he told me to go and he assured me that he would still be there when I got back. That was hard being away at that time, but I did go and when I came back, he was still with us.

My family has always been a priority but my dad's health was really unstable near the end and I wasn't at a point in my life that I could stop everything and stay by his side. He knew I was always there for him and proved to me time and time again that he was a fighter in every sense of the word. I guess that's where I get that from!

## This One's for You Dad!

More dirt road memories about my dad . . . The Outdoor Channel holds an awards show every January for their television personalities and producers, which is called the Golden Moose Awards or GMAs. Melissa and I attended our first GMA in 2010. We were sitting in the very back in the nosebleed section, when I noticed that a lot of other television shows were up front in the VIP section. I asked an employee with Outdoor Channel, "How do we get up there," and she told me that our show needed to be nominated for a GMA to get the VIP passes. I thought to myself, "Okay. Now I know what I need to do."

That night, I watched a lot of our friends walk across the stage and get a GMA. I got even more frustrated as the night went on. I wasn't mad at the winners because as far as I was concerned, they all deserved an award. I was mad at myself because we didn't even submit any of our shows for the GMAs. It's hard to get nominated if you don't even enter.

The next year in January 2011, we entered and got nominated. We even got to sit at table number one in the VIP section. I soon found out that just because you're at table number one, doesn't mean that you WON. But we were definitely closer to getting on that stage and winning a GMA.

You know how when you attend something like this, the first thing your parents want to know when you return home is if you won? My dad said, "Well, did you win one of those Golden Moose thingies?" I really hated to tell him because I didn't want to let him down. I said "No Dad. We didn't win this year." He didn't miss a beat and reassured us by saying, "Don't worry. You'll get 'em next year." My dad passed away on December 22, 2011. His funeral was the day after Christmas.

On January 19, 2012, Melissa and I went back to the GMAs for round three. This time we were walking across that stage in Las Vegas, Nevada with the rest of our staff at the 12th Annual Golden Moose Awards and accepted our very FIRST Golden Moose Award for Best Off-Road Series on Outdoor Channel.

If we never win another award, I would be cool with that because that Golden Moose Award meant more to me than any other award we'll ever win. I stood on the stage that evening and accepted our award with my team by my side and at the end of my acceptance speech, I said, "This one's for you DAD!"

If you want something, you have to go after it! It won't just come to you. We had to enter to WIN and that's just what we did!

# CHAPTER 7

## Navigating the Road Together: Building a Booming Business with Your Spouse

I am asked all the time how my wife and I work so well together in business. To tell you the truth, I couldn't imagine it any other way. Melissa is EVERYTHING to me—my best friend, business partner, confidant, wife and mother of my children. I know she always has my back just as much as I have hers. We have it "together, together" if that makes sense. We consider each other teammates in business and life and it's us against the world. We have totally opposite personalities and are both very competitive. I think that's what I love about her most. She keeps me on my toes and motivates me. Everything from exercising to racing go-karts, she challenges me to do more to win, pushing us both to be the best we can be.

I met Melissa right after I graduated high school in 1987. You could say her life had been less than normal growing up. Her father was an abusive alcoholic and her mother lived in fear of him. That was the type of life Melissa was accustomed to. She was nothing like her family. There was something very special about her.

The people who raised me were actually my grandparents, which wasn't a problem, but having raised three children of their own already, I'm sure starting over with me was somewhat of a challenge.

Melissa and I definitely didn't get to where we are with any kind of advantages. We earned every bit of what we have together, but that's okay, we wouldn't have it any other way. We both had a lot to learn about relationships from the get-go.

## Figuring Out What's "Right"

Two important qualities for me in the beginning of our relationship was being on time and being honest, both of which were big problems for Melissa. She was late for everything. I'm not talking fifteen to twenty minutes. I'm talking an hour or two hours. It was bad. She would also tell little white lies about something that really didn't matter, which would lead to having to tell another lie and another lie. Looking back, I realize that's what she learned growing up. Fortunately, she figured out that it was wrong and worked on making some changes.

I was not perfect by any means either. I guess you could say I was an introvert and very hotheaded at times. But just like Melissa, I was willing and able to work on those things. Regardless, we both accepted the fact that we were not perfect and agreed to meet in the middle with what we felt was the "right" way to do things. I think that's what makes a relationship work—communication and the willingness to change and/or meet in the middle. The MLM business that we got involved in helped us with some of these lessons. We read a lot of self-help books and started applying them to our daily lives. Something as simple as reading a book with an open mind can lead your life in a different direction.

Over the years we've learned the importance of keeping our relationship as our first priority. That means being respectful and thinking of your partner's feelings before doing something that might harm your relationship. This is easy to do if you put yourself in the other person's shoes and think of how you would feel if that same thing were done or said to you. This is also a good practice for building a stronger family. Treat other people the way you would want to be treated.

Another important element to a good relationship and family life is showing love and saying, "I love you." Don't be afraid to express your feelings and show you care. We have a really close family, and that's because we always put family first. They are not second on my list of priorities. We make it a point to sit down and have dinner together on a regular basis. All of our cell phones are put away at that time so we can communicate over dinner. I think quality time is an important element many families are missing now. This is just one example of how we reconnect and stay close. How do you make your family a priority?

## Down But Not Out

Our first five years together were challenging as with any new relationship. We were both very strong willed and hard headed so we had lots of things to figure out. I worked at the printing company and Melissa was employed as a paralegal in a law office.

We got married in 1992 and had three children. Life was a challenge every step of the way just to keep food in the refrigerator. Our real struggle with money began after our first child was born when we decided Melissa would quit her job to stay at home to raise our children. To say we were broke doesn't really describe it. Ramen noodles with peanut butter and jelly sandwiches were a common meal for us. We were on the edge of bankruptcy many times and received notice after notice of foreclosure on our front door, which was then followed up by numerous threatening phone calls. We never blamed one another for our position with our finances because living on one income was a mutual decision between us. Not having enough money and not being able to pay the bills are some of the biggest stresses on relationships. This will make you or break you when it comes right down to it.

A good lesson we learned is that it is easier and less stressful to stay in communication with bill collectors than to ignore them and run. If bill collectors are calling you, answer the call and make arrangements even if it's something small. No one can fault someone when they are making an effort. Somehow we pulled through because no matter what, we were always on the same team and stayed focused on what we had, rather than what we didn't.

## The Decision to Work Together

I knew Melissa was really smart, so I wanted her to come work with me when she was ready to go back to work after the kids were in school. I couldn't see her working for others to help fulfill their goals and dreams. We tried a lot of different business ideas and failed many times over! I don't know if you would say we failed or just hit a wall and then quit to look for a different business idea that might work faster. Regardless, we didn't have it in us to give up. It wasn't until my meeting with the local millionaire where he talked to me about staying focused that our lives took a turn for the better.

I used to tell Melissa that we were going to have a beautiful 5,000 square foot home on fifty acres with a big pole barn full of toys (ATVs, boat, etc.) and that she would have a nice car so that she wouldn't have to worry about breaking down or running out of gas. I kept the dream in front of us. It is important to set goals as a team and not just individually. Her goals were not always the same as mine, but we did find some common ground on a few, which is one of the reasons we pushed each other to work so hard.

## Personal Time versus Business Time

Having your own business can be very challenging, maybe even more so when you're in business with your spouse. How many times have you heard people complain about their spouse bringing work home with them? When I say bringing work home, I mean the negativity and gossip about everything that happened at work that day. It's important to know when to call it a day and turn work off. I know some people have a real problem with this, but you have to have a good balance in life to maintain a great relationship.

When you work with your spouse, sometimes this can be even more difficult because you lose sight of the difference between personal time and business time. Know when enough is enough. Yeah we eat, sleep, and breathe our business, but it's still refreshing to have a life outside of that. We found ourselves working together 24/7, so there wasn't much free time. It was important to our business and personal life for each of us to take a day here and there to do whatever made us happy. For Melissa, that might mean hanging out with friends or going shopping. For me, it was going for a ride or going hunting. This "understanding" helped us keep it together, together in business and life.

Another thing we do that many married-with-children couples don't do enough is schedule date night every week. Just keeping that balance in our lives is important to our relationship as husband and wife. That's when we try not to talk about business and enjoy some of the rewards of working so hard. Sometimes focusing on your spouse is really difficult, especially when you are truly passionate about the work you are doing. But you must commit to non-business-related time together.

## Stay in Your Lane

After I quit my full-time job and we started working the dealership together, Melissa and I were now a team, and we found ourselves up against some new business challenges. We realized that she was not good with the books/accounting so we hired someone to help with that. I found I couldn't do sales and work on our ATVs and be efficient, so we hired a few mechanics. You need to figure out where you can be the most effective inside your business and stick with it.

Sometimes it's hard to let certain things go and entrust them to someone else, especially when you know you could do it better. No one cares about your business as much as you do or you both do. That's just a reality. By having someone else help out, even if it's not exactly the way you would do it, can take a lot of stress off of you. This allows you to focus on what you need to do to move forward.

Here's a crazy example but a good one. We live in Tennessee and have about ten acres of grass to mow every week for at least seven to eight months out of the year. With the television show and speaking engagements, there wasn't much free time in my schedule. It would take me almost a full day to mow the lawn, and my wife kept after me to have our sixteen-year-old son help me with it.

Finally, I took her advice and had our son Brady help out. It drove me crazy because he would run over rocks, have lots of high spots, miss some areas, and so on. It was definitely not done the way I would have done it, but the reality of it was, it *was* getting mowed each week and I could direct him with changes and within a few weeks, he had it mastered.  By letting someone else take care of this task, I gave myself back one full day each week to focus on what I needed to be doing. My time was much more valuable than sitting on my mower a full day out of each week. This is how I learned that it's okay to let go so you can stay focused on what you're good at and what's important to your business.

Figure out what your strong qualities are and focus on them. Don't try to do it all. That's why you have a business partner. Melissa and I have different talents, which we realize and use to build each other up. We complement each other by being different but somewhat the same.

When we had our dealership, we had a lot of men come into the store that would only come to me for advice when it came to buying or repairing their ATV. Now I knew that Melissa was smart when it came to this stuff, because she grew up in the country and had been riding her entire life. She was also in charge of our parts and service at the dealership, so she reviewed service orders with our technicians and was on the computer looking up parts every day. I started seeing what was going on, so when someone would come in and pass by Melissa to talk to me about fixing their ATV or SXS, I would tell them I didn't know and send them over to Melissa for help. It didn't take long;

customers started coming in and going right to her for help. Don't be afraid to give each other credit. It will help you with time management, give you a sense of pride, and give you each valuable roles to fill in the business.

Melissa was also good with writing letters because she had worked in a law office for five years. Everyone in the office called her the "word queen." I was not as good so I would have her proofread all my letters and emails before sending them out, and eventually I caught on to what she was looking for.

Now on the other hand, she was always smiling and never good with confrontation so I was the one who had to deal with the staff and being the bad guy, if need be. Figure out your roles in your business and stick with what you're good at.

## No Limit to Your Capabilities

When we started the TV show, we still had the dealership, so we were working double time. We both had a very good work ethic, which worked to our benefit, so putting in the time was not a problem. I started traveling a lot to film, and Melissa would stay back to run the dealership. She was used to me being around her all the time, so being away from each other was not easy.

It wasn't long before Melissa came to me and told me that she wanted to get involved and travel with me. She said she was going to learn how to run a video camera. Now I have to tell you that her video skills were the worst I've ever seen. She would video using the screen and talk to everyone while she was videoing and the end result—Blair Witch footage. You couldn't watch any of our home movies without getting sick! I challenged her and told her I didn't think she could do it. She rose to the occasion and taught herself video and production. Now, she is the BEST video/production person we have. This just proves you can do anything if you really put your mind to it!

Having Melissa with me on the road and behind the camera gives me confidence because I know she cares about our business and has my best interest in mind. I never have to worry if we got all the shots we needed or what she is saying to a partner or viewer out on the road. She's not afraid to give me her opinion or help me with direction in production either which is very helpful when I'm in front of the camera.

## Believing in Each Other

Making a change in business is very difficult and the possibilities can scare you, but if it's something you're passionate about, it's really helpful to have your copilot on board. Our switch from the dealership to television took some convincing. It definitely didn't happen overnight. With my record, Melissa knew how easily I had changed direction in the past, and she was trying to keep me focused. This is when being open-minded can really pay off. Sometimes you just have to run on faith and be open to change. I had no experience with television but once I showed Melissa how serious I was about the television career, she believed in me and never once told me that I couldn't do it.

She is my biggest supporter and worked just as hard as me to see it happen. Believing in one another is so important to a relationship, especially if you're in business together. We knew there was nothing we couldn't do, if we believed and put our minds to it. You get out of life and relationships what you put into them, which is why we always put "us" first.

## It Could Always Be Worse

As a couple, it is important not to lose focus on what is really important because that can help you power through the tough times. I have to share this story with you because it gave me a whole different perspective on the challenges I was facing. One day Melissa was cleaning out the attic and getting rid of some of our stuff as she loves to do. She had some guy come by the office to pick up a bunch of boxes. What I didn't know is that she had just gotten rid of the riding gear that I had worn on our very first show without asking me. I was furious!

I went outside to blow off some steam and get away from her when I noticed my neighbor Earl standing outside in his driveway. I thought to myself, *I'm going to go tell Earl what she did and he will surely agree with me*. I walked over and before I even got up to him, he looked up at me and I could see he was crying. His eyes and face were all red. I knew something major was wrong. I said, "What's up Earl?" He looked at me and said sadly "I'm not sure how much longer I'm going to be your neighbor."

I thought it was about money and I was about to ask how much he needed, but before I could even say a word, he said, "I just found out my wife has cancer and only has a few months to live." He told me that his kids were on their way over at that very moment so he could tell them. All of a sudden that riding gear didn't matter to me anymore. What was happening with Earl and his wife made me sit back and take a good hard look at what I had instead of what I didn't.

One of my favorite sayings is, "It could always be worse." Thinking about Earl and his family, that idea just hit me hard. So then, like a good husband, I went in to my wife and told her how much I loved her and that I was sorry I acted like an ass. Sometimes we get so hung up on the little things that we miss out on the good stuff in life.

## Protect What's Yours

Melissa and I are always mindful of showing respect especially when we're around other people. We have a mutual agreement that when we have anything to discuss or a disagreement, we will address it when we are alone and not in the company of others. We also never undermine one another in any way, shape, or form. That is completely disrespectful. If it ever does happen by chance, we will talk about it when we are alone and work everything out.

You should never air your feelings out on social media or talk behind each other's back. That word gets around quickly because most people want to see you fail so you'll stay on their level or below them in life. Always keep the best interest of the company in mind with every decision you make and protect your company, no matter what.

Remember, you're on the same team so it's your job to keep each other's spirits up, especially in difficult times. And if you have your own business, there will be difficult times. You can't afford to both be down on the same days. That could cost you a lot of time and money. Believe in each other and support one another. Fortunately, our mutual trust and support was a big help in building our business in the beginning when we were going through our tax situation.

Some days you just don't feel like keeping your head above water, but one of you has to stay positive and focused on where you're going, not where you are. Most tough situations are just temporary roadblocks that you have to find your way around. In our relationship, one of us is always ready to lift the other up as needed. That's what having a GREAT team is about!

## Communication Is Key

Communicate. Communicate. Communicate. This is probably the most important piece of advice when you have a business with your spouse. Talk to each other about what is going on and what might be bothering you. Do this on a daily basis. Don't let things build up into an uncomfortable conflict. Keeping an open line of communication with your spouse or partner is an important element to your success in business. This also helps you both stay positive and moving in the right direction.

Most people can't read minds. I say most, because, after you've been with someone for a long time, you do start to think, say, and do things exactly the same. It can be kind of freaky sometimes because your partner may say something that you are thinking or pick a restaurant that you've been thinking of going to but haven't visited for awhile. Melissa and I do this all the time and to the point that nothing surprises me.

Once we started making money, we came to an agreement that if anything cost more than $1,000, we would discuss it before we make the purchase. Get in the habit of making decisions together, especially large decisions. If you can't reach an agreement, give it some time and think about it, but keep the lines of communication open. Laughter is something I think is pretty important to good communication. Don't be afraid to do something silly to make each other laugh. That's what makes a good relationship great!

No matter how hard you are chasing your dream, you need to take time out to get away and recharge your batteries. You may look at this as unnecessary and say you don't have the time or need a break, but trust me. I was the worst for thinking that very same way. Taking breaks gives you a chance to sit back and look at your business from the outside in. This is really hard for real go-getters, but it is something that you need to make happen, even if it's just a camping trip or going to the lake for the day to sit back and relax. This is not only great for your relationship, but it's great for your health too.

Having your spouse in business with you can be very rewarding. You're both in the trenches together, fighting the fight to reach your goals and dreams. You fail together but you win together! That's the reward. Melissa and I started at the bottom together and have been through hell and back. We've had lots of ups and downs and twists and turns along the way, but all those challenges and adversities have made us stronger and I wouldn't change our journey, even if I could.

## You Need a Great Team to Win

We've learned a lot from working together as husband and wife over the years. There is no doubt that you get out of life whatever you put into it. Surrounding yourself with a great team of people in your business is just as important as having it together, together as husband and wife.

No one really cares as much as you do when it comes to the success of your own business. And although that is true, there are still individuals out there who are passionate about being a team player and doing a great job. You just need to find them and then maximize your team's strengths!

We always view our staff as our team and try never to use the words "I" "ME" or "EMPLOYEES." Everything we do is a team effort, working together toward the same goals and sharing credit in our accomplishments. There is no "I" in "TEAM" and there is no room in business for an "I" "ME" kind of person. People come up to me on the road and tell me how much they like "my" show. What they fail to realize is that it is "our" show, because without the team of people (videographers, producers, editors, partners, etc.) behind the scenes that make me look good and put it all together, none of it would be possible.

Our very first editor for our show was an "I" "ME" person. We were struggling just to pay network fees and get things off the ground. My goal was to always take care of our team and the network fees to keep us on the air before we would pay ourselves. As I mentioned earlier, we were selling our dealership on a three-year sales agreement so income completely depended on sponsorship dollars, which our editor knew going into the project. This editor was constantly after me using the words "I" and "ME" and that did nothing but piss me off.

During one particular week, we were waiting on a check to arrive, and I told her that we wouldn't be able to pay her until Monday. It wasn't that I *wasn't* going to pay her, it was just going to be a few days later. She immediately flipped and went into her typical "I" "ME" conversation, so I let her go. As far as I was concerned, she was not a team player and would only bring negativity to our team. When I told Melissa, she said, "What are we going to do? She was our only editor." I responded with my usual, "I'll figure it out," and I did. Not even one week later we had a new editor with a whole lot more talent sitting in her chair. I never let someone's level of talent control my decision of replacing them. There is always someone better out there. You just have to find them.

An NFL quarterback gets all the recognition, but he knows that he can't win without his team. He doesn't show up to play on game day without practicing with his team and preparing every day to win. Without the front line holding off the opponent's defense, the quarterback and running backs can't get their jobs done. When Emmitt Smith #22 played for the Dallas Cowboys, he bought all the players on his offensive line a Rolex watch because he knew that without them blocking for him, he never would have achieved as many rushing yards. There is usually a "front person," but there's always a "team" pulling it all together for the win!

A few years ago, Melissa and I were special guests of an auto manufacturer to attend a NASCAR race in Virginia. On our way over to the track, we found ourselves in an elevator at the hotel with a NASCAR pit crew. There was one particular gentleman in the elevator that day who seemed to be having a really bad day, venting about how they had four more races to go and he was tired of it and wanted to go home. He was just bringing the entire team down. Now, since we had talked with the team briefly in the elevator, they were on my mind, so I watched how they performed at the race that day. Unfortunately, this team had terrible performance the entire day with the worst pit times of everyone and didn't finish the race due to a mechanical issue with the car. My guess is the reason they had issues with the car is because that one gentleman in the elevator had worked so hard at bringing down the entire team.

## Pulling Weeds

There were actually a few instances when we had this type of person on our team, which could have caused real devastation if we had not taken action. We always knew it was important to take time for staff meetings and personal celebrations like holidays and birthdays to keep our team close and help build a strong foundation. I recall one particular team member that we hired who came from a very corporate world and didn't like our "team bonding." He started acting as if it were a bother, rushing everyone, like he had more important things to do. Eventually, our team started to fall apart, and we were not working together the way we should. It didn't take long for us to realize that it was time for him to go. We needed to "pull the weeds" to let the garden grow.

Weeds are plants that are growing out of place, and they can be a serious garden problem because they rob vegetable plants of sunlight, water, and nutrients. It is important to control weeds when they are small and before they get out of control. Consider your staff your garden. It only takes one bad weed to start taking over your dedicated team of people.

In business, this is sometimes difficult to deal with, especially if it's a good friend, family member, or someone who's been there for a very long time. But this is where you need to focus on your company, how this person is affecting it, and where you will be in the next year if you don't take control. You might look at it and think well it's only one person and we really need them because they're good at what they do. But if they aren't a team player and bringing positivity to the team, they need to go. Remember, everything happens for a reason. In most cases, we found someone better who could do the same job.

Speaking of pulling weeds, a few years back, we were on a shoot in Louisiana with a company that makes aftermarket accessories for the powersports industry. Part of their sales pitch is providing great customer service. We were standing by the front receptionist desk to get a good b-roll shot to promote great customer service with the receptionist answering the phone in a friendly tone, "Hello, how can I help you?" When the phone finally rang, it was 5:01 p.m. The receptionist looked at the owner and said, "It's 5:01 p.m. and I'm not getting that." This is the same girl who had shown up ten minutes late for work that very same day. If it were my business, I would have pulled that weed a long time ago.

## Commit to Your Business

Being a business owner or in a management position can be very difficult, especially when someone is not pulling his or her weight. We had a cameraman working on our team a few years back who was supposed to be filming with Keystone RV at our annual off-road event, Fisher's ATV Reunion. This was our fifth year, and we had over twenty acres of vendors attending our four-day event with many prominent companies present.

This particular year, we had finally made a connection with the world's largest towable RV manufacturer, Keystone RV, and they agreed to display a few of their popular toy hauler units at our event. The deal: they would pay us $10,000 to produce a ten minute video at our event for use in all their dealerships. Now the cameraman that I was referring to earlier only had one job, which was to film with them over this four-day period.

A few weeks later, we went into post-production to review the footage and there was very little footage for us to use to put this video together. I was furious. There was no way we could give them a good ten minute video with what we had, so I called our contact at Keystone RV and discussed the situation with him. I then asked if Melissa and I could visit and tour their facility to do some more filming to get the video done. He couldn't believe that we were willing to do this.

We made arrangements and drove the ten hours, had our visit and filmed, and then we returned back to the office and completed the video. They loved it! As a matter of fact, Keystone RV signed a six-figure deal with us all because of the commitment we showed them. It was the first time in the company's history to ever do something like this. This wasn't just another story for us to "Go Beyond Average" but a story to represent the commitment that Melissa and I feel to our company and our team. Needless to say, it wasn't long before that cameraman was looking for work elsewhere.

Whether you own your own business or work for someone else, always think of it as your own and consider what you would do if you were paying the bills. If you're that employee who's always looking to stick it to the company, you'll never get ahead. Sitting around trying to figure out how much vacation time, sick time, personal time, salary, bonuses, company vehicle, and any other perks you can suck out of the company is SMALL-time thinking and will always result in SMALL-time salaries.

If you want to be making $50,000, $100,000, $200,000 or even a million, then you need to start working like you're making it. Don't be one of those people who say, "I'm giving them exactly what they're paying me for" or "They don't pay me enough to do that." If you think that way, then that's all you'll ever be making. You'll only get paid for the work you're doing. You won't get a bonus or a raise by anticipating that you'll work harder. Start giving more and you will get more. Supposedly, an estimated $650 billion a year is wasted on workplace distractions. TEAM players who put in the work and treat the company as their own will always move ahead in the business world.

# CHAPTER 8

## Expect Detours
## (Comfort Zone & Sacrifice)

No matter what path you take in life, there will always be detours. Everything doesn't go as planned. That's just a fact of life. But that doesn't keep you from getting what you are going after. It just means you might have to take another route to get there. I've had lots of detours but kept pushing forward. Some of the biggest roadblocks that led us down a different path turned out to have some of the greatest rewards at the end. Don't get frustrated when life reroutes you to a different path. A little faith and perseverance is just what you need. You see, that's the difference between a winner and a loser. Losers give up but winners push on.

### Be Uncomfortable

If you're living in a comfort zone, you're not moving forward. For me, it was really uncomfortable in the beginning to call on companies to "sponsor" our television show, especially given the fact that I really didn't have any experience in doing this sort of thing.

The reality of it was: I had to make myself uncomfortable in order to be successful. If it was going to be, it was up to me. No one was going to do it for me. I had to believe in myself before I could get others to have faith in me.

Many times I had to suck it up and dig deep to get out of my comfort zone and do the unthinkable. Remember, I was the total introvert, with no communication skills, the hotheaded guy who wasn't good with people, but I knew that I wanted more, and I was willing to do whatever it took to get it. I needed to take a chance and put myself out there. No guts, no glory. When I put myself under pressure, I found I did my best work, which in turn led to the best victories.

I was also uncomfortable being in front of the camera. That took some getting used to. As I mentioned earlier, the hardest part was going back and watching myself on camera. Over the years, this got much easier for me and now I love it. I'm always pushing myself to do things that make me uncomfortable because I know that's what I need to grow. If you believe in yourself, you'll see it through until others start believing in you.

When our television show started to really take off, I was invited to emcee some pretty major events. This was all new to me, something I had never done before.

I had no idea how to emcee in front of thousands of people, but I knew there are great rewards in being uncomfortable.

One of my first experiences with emceeing an event was for the country music industry at the CMA Fest (aka Fan Fair) in Nashville, Tennessee. We were invited to hold our very own ATV Rodeo in the Tennessee Titans parking lot during Fan Fair. We had twelve well-known country music artists compete in our ATV Rodeo for a chance to win two new Suzuki ATVs. I was on stage hosting the entire thing as they competed. Everything came together and we pulled off a very successful event. Actually, the CMA told us that our ATV Rodeo was a huge hit in retaining attendance and invited us back again, but we declined due to the logistics, time, and money that it took to pull it all together.

My next big event was emceeing on stage at the Country Stampede in Manhattan, Kansas, with over 125,000 people in attendance. Melissa was so nervous for me that she was sick to her stomach. As I was heading up on stage, she asked me, "What are you going to say?" I said, "I don't know but I'll figure it out." I pushed myself to get out of my comfort zone that day and felt great accomplishment in knowing that I had done it. At that very moment, I fell in love with being in front of people and entertaining them.

It wasn't long until we started putting on our own events where I would host and emcee in front of thousands of people throughout an entire weekend. I truly love the rush of being on stage. Now just imagine if I had initially declined to host the CMA Fest ATV Rodeo. I would have missed out on this amazing, life-changing opportunity.

## Embrace Failure

If you ask people who are really successful how they did it, a common answer will be "I failed a lot." Failing can mean many things such as not hitting a goal, getting the word "No," getting a divorce, taking a wrong road in life, and so on. In any event, you only lose if you don't get back up. No one is perfect, so consider your failures as lessons in life. You have to fail to succeed. Every time I got a no from potential television partners, I felt a sense of relief because I knew I was one step closer to a yes. I could then cross that person off my list and go after another partner. I knew that it was all a numbers game and that I would eventually get a yes. Learn to embrace failure. It means you're progressing.

Think about this, when a child learns to walk, they fall down over and over again. How do they learn to walk? They keep getting back up. Some of the best athletes in history have the greatest stories of failing first. Take for instance Michael Jordan, cut from his high school basketball team, or Babe Ruth, known for his home run record (714 during his career) but who had 1,330 strikeouts, which was the record for strikeouts for decades.

We have always approached life with the attitude of "anything is possible if you put your mind to it" and used common phrases such as "It could always be worse" or my favorite, "I'll figure it out." Working toward similar goals really helped. Melissa and I are on the same page as far as doing whatever it takes and believing in one another.

## Take the Road Less Traveled

Everyone has to start somewhere and we never lived beyond our means. Neither one of us felt the need to buy things just to impress other people. We didn't care what others thought of us, as long as we were happy. We practiced delayed gratification and made many sacrifices, doing things that others were not willing to do. Some of these included driving old crappy vehicles; rescheduling a holiday celebration or birthday party due to work or a business commitment; missing a game, school event, or friend's party; driving long distances to pick up ATVs on nights that I had to work the next morning at the printing company, and so on. We were willing to go down those roads because we knew where we were going.

## Put It On a Shelf

We've experienced detours both in business and personally throughout the years, but giving up was never an option. We went through some things on a personal level in our lives that would have definitely broken many people. It has not been an easy road. That's why our story is the *Dirt Road to Success*. I learned early on that it's not what happens to you; it's how you react to it.

Whenever we were going through some setback or disappointment in our personal lives, we never let that affect our business and vice versa. We "put it on a shelf" so to speak and left it there while we took care of whatever we had to at that time. We knew it would still be there on the shelf when we returned. This gave us time to clear our minds and be able to deal with whatever it was when we were ready. This simple concept has helped push us through some truly tough times. All people go through hardships at one time or another in their lives. You need to learn to separate what's personal and what's business and deal with each accordingly so they do not affect one another.

## Think Ahead

It's a good idea to always think ahead in business, kind of like teaching our kids how to drive. If you see a sharp corner coming up or need to turn onto a different route, you have to prepare yourself for that move. When I was teaching our youngest son Brady how to drive, he would always speed up when he came into a corner. I would tell him to, "Prepare for what's ahead and brake into the corner then accelerate out." Thinking ahead, in business and in life, can help you avoid accidents and keep you on the road. I always tried to look three moves ahead and think about how each decision I made that day would affect me three to six months down the road.

A perfect example of this was how we did not burn any bridges with the Outdoor Channel programming department the first time we were kicked off the air. This meant we had somewhere to return to when things didn't work out on the network we had moved to. Always think of what changes might come down the road. Sometimes the people you are dealing with move to a different position or get fired, so it's a good idea to keep other options in mind.

## Give It Your Laser Focus

You need to learn to deal with only what's in front of you at that time. Focus on ONE thing. Whatever project/task you are working on should be the only thing you focus on until you're done. Give it your laser focus and you will get it completed to its fullest potential. Your undivided attention makes you more productive and more effective because you know you are doing it the right way. If I say I'm going to do three emails for sponsorships, organize my tool box, cut the lawn, do a few standups, review footage for the show, get cameras together, and so on, I won't get everything accomplished to its fullest potential. What would you rather have done: ten things half-assed or three things 100 percent correct?

We met with an executive from a major company a few years back and I asked why he never responded to any of my emails. He told me that he was overloaded with 3,500 emails in his inbox so he had decided to move them all to a "3,500 folder" and start over. His theory was that the people who really wanted to get in touch with him would email him again. I don't know that I would have done this but you could look at this one of two ways: He was either being irresponsible or he was giving his laser focus to what was most important and staying on top of it. If you're on the other end of this deal, that's a perfect example of why persistence is vital to your success.

## Learn to Say No

Sometimes focus is about learning to say "No." Melissa has a habit of always over extending herself when it comes to school functions, dinner dates, friend favors, and so on. I have to actually step in and help her say "No" so we can stay focused on what we are doing. If you're not careful, distractions like this can consume all your time and energy if you let it. Now, don't get me wrong, I don't mind giving back some of our time or taking some time away from work, but if you don't have a good balance, your focus will go off the trail and you'll find yourself down the wrong road, requiring more time to get to your destination.

If a friend asks you to give him some of your time to help out with a project, you would more than likely say yes. But if he asks you to give him $5,000 to help with a project, you would probably say "Hell No!" Why are you willing to give them the most valuable thing you have that you can't replace, but yet you won't consider giving them money, which is the one thing that can be replaced? The problem here is that we don't put a value on our time. Do you have any idea what your time is worth?

# CHAPTER 9

## Tips for the Road (Friends, Be Healthy, Dress for Success, & Customer Service)

When I say, "go beyond average," what's the first thing that pops into your head? Is it being different or doing things differently than your peers? Is it how you treat people or how you live? Is it going against the grain or taking the road less traveled? Is it not being like everyone around you? To tell you the truth, it means all of those things. This is something that really made a difference in our lives from the beginning. We didn't want to settle for being average. There were people out there living the type of life we wanted to live. Why not us? You will only have and do what you feel worthy of, which is why you might need to raise your self-worth in order to have more.

Being a leader or in business is no easy street. It requires you to go beyond average. There is always something to do, someone to meet, a decision to be made, etc. To be successful, it's important to not only believe in yourself but also prepare yourself mentally, physically, and emotionally to take on anything that comes your way. Having a good balance of mind, body, and spirit is essential to your success. Many people think money is the key to success, but in reality, it is balance. When you find a good balance, you will find true happiness in all that you are.

## The Circle of Friends

When I worked at the printing company, we had friends who went to the bar and partied every weekend. Don't get me wrong, I do like to have a good time, but I couldn't see myself doing that every single weekend. That just wasn't for me. I knew that if I wanted more out of life, I had to do more. I had to go beyond average. People say you become like the people you hang out with on a regular basis. Through reading self-help books, I realized that we needed to make a few new friends. Your income and lifestyle will be a reflection of your five closest friends' income and lifestyle. Who are the friends in your circle? Could it be time to make some changes?

## It's What You Do Every Day

Daily habits play a big part in whether you are a success or failure. What changes can you make in your life to help you become better in your personal and business life? For me, reading self-help books has really catapulted me in my career and life. I try to feed my brain every day by reading and listening to other successful people. When I go into a meeting, I listen with an open mind and do less talking, especially when I'm with a very successful businessperson. Sometimes you can be so focused on other things and what you're going to say next, that you never fully take in what is put in front of you. Keep the positive flowing in and the positive will continue to flow out.

## Stay Healthy

Staying healthy also makes you perform at peak levels and feel confident in yourself. You can lose a lot of productive time by being sick. That's why it's important to get plenty of rest, eat right, and exercise on a daily basis. Consider your body your one and only vehicle in life. You need to take care of it. Work on making YOU better. That's a step in the right direction in going beyond average!

Being overweight can work against you both mentally and physically. Stress can easily put that weight on, but on the up side, exercise relieves stress so why wouldn't you make time to do it? Even if you find time to go for a short walk, something is better than nothing. This also gives you time to clear your head so you can think better. Some people like to work out in the mornings, but Melissa and I found that we work best doing office work in the mornings right after breakfast and then exercise after dinner. This helps us get done what we need to right away and then relieve the stress later.

One thing I do to stay healthy is wash my hands a lot. I meet many people and shake plenty of hands out on the road and I can't tell you how many times I've seen grown men leave the bathroom without washing their hands. I'm sure there are a lot of women who also fall into this same category. It only takes a minute to wash your hands. For you guys and gals who do wash your hands while you're using a public restroom, be sure to use the towel you dried your hands off with to open the bathroom door because that's where all the germs are found from the people who aren't washing their hands.

## Avoid Drinking Too Much

Another good pointer for you in taking care of yourself, especially on business trips, is don't drink too much. This could cause you to do or say things you'll regret down the road. I never drink more than one or two beers when I'm conducting business or in a dinner meeting. If you follow this simple rule, you can learn a lot about the person or company you're with by just listening, especially when they're drinking more than they should.

One of our close friends shared a tip when she is on the road in business meetings; she orders her first drink (gin and tonic or something similar that is clear) and then secretly lets the bartender know that she is the designated driver so when she goes back to the bar, she asks for her usual and they give her water with a lime or lemon. This could be very useful, especially if you have someone who is really pushing you to drink.

## Dress for Success/Hygiene

When I started dealing with more professional people in my career, I realized that I needed some help with my wardrobe and style to know what was "in." I did some research online and found a couple men's specialty stores that helped me coordinate a few outfits as well as pair them with the right shoes. They can also help with color coordination, size, proper fit, and give you great tips as well as advice on new trends. You want to look as good as you can, because the better you look, the better you feel.

For all you guys, there is nothing like a fresh haircut, clean shave, and clean clothes. Be sure to check for nose hair, ear hair, and wandering eyebrows too. And for goodness sakes guys, trim your fingernails. It's funny because we joke about this at our house with designated days like Fingernail Friday and Toenail Tuesday.

If you are uncomfortable with your smile, don't be afraid to get your teeth fixed or have your teeth whitened. These are personal things that can hold you back from your true potential and will have a big effect on how you feel about yourself. Sometimes these little things can cost you a sale, account, job interview, date, or whatever you are going after.

This one is going to hit some of you hard. If you're a smoker and you meet with a non-smoker for a meeting, interview, or to set up a new account, you're already up against a wall because if they are one of those people who are offended by someone who smells like an ashtray, you probably won't make out so well. Stack the odds in your favor and don't smoke a cigarette right before your meeting. It also wouldn't hurt to take your toothbrush along so you can freshen up before your meeting.

## Express Yourself

According to the University of Pennsylvania, it only takes a person five to ten seconds to form an impression of you. Fifty-five percent of the impression people form about you is based on your posture, body movements, and gestures, while 38 percent is based on the tone of your voice, and only 7 percent is based on what you say.

I can always tell how confident people are by their handshake. There is nothing like someone looking you in the eye and delivering a good firm handshake. That automatically gives you a certain level of trust and confidence in the person. If this is something you don't have, it is definitely something you should work on.

Another way to go beyond average is to smile and be happy. How many people do you come across throughout the day who are quick to dump all their negative crap on you? If you allow this, they will keep doing it. It's better to steer clear of putting yourself in those situations. If someone starts being negative, just change the subject and move on. Having a positive attitude can make all the difference in everything around you. People are attracted to happy people so why not set the odds in your favor to open the many doors put in front of you by staying positive. If you're not a "people person," then don't get a job or business where you have to deal with people. It's that simple.

## The Customer Experience

I know I mentioned how we went beyond average and used rapport in our dealership earlier and then also used that same concept as we dealt with our partners for our television show. No matter what business you are in, having a good customer experience, can keep your business moving in the right direction.

Here's a good example of what not to do: I stopped by a local service shop to have some work done on one of our vehicles. This was my first time visiting this shop, so my customer service radar was on high alert. As soon as I walked in, I could feel tension with the guy at the service counter. He was on the phone rolling his eyes as a customer was trying to set up a service appointment. I scanned the room and noticed a sticky note on the wall that read "Let me drop everything I'm doing so I can listen to your problem." The door was open to the service area and I could hear the technicians talking loud and being extremely vulgar. Once the counter guy was off the phone, I tried to explain my problem and get a service appointment, but he acted as if my basic request was a big bother to him. Needless to say, that was the last time I ever stepped into that place.

I tip at restaurants on the service I'm given, not what they say the standard is. I've left some really great tips but have also left some really bad tips because of the service I was provided. Good service always pays well and bad service, well, not so well. For me, it only takes one bad experience to make a decision to never go back and to take my business elsewhere.

Our daughter, Briana, was a waitress at Buffalo Wild Wings. Many evenings she would come home with tips of a few hundred dollars. This didn't happen by chance. She was very good at what she did and understood the importance of building rapport with her customers. She told us just by knowing someone's name, their order, or something more personal from their last visit made her customers feel special. They would always return and ask for her. This is yet another example of going beyond average.

Melissa and I had flights to the other side of the country that were purchased through a corporate partner. Now most corporate companies use a travel agency to book the flights and don't take the time to pick out your seats so, on this flight, Melissa and I were placed on opposite ends of the plane, both in middle seats. We attempted to get a seat change at the kiosk with no luck.

When we tried to go up to the ticket counter, a rude staff member kept directing us to the kiosk because they were not taking anyone at the counter for seat changes. We were frustrated.

After a while the staff person left her post and my wife asked a gentleman at the counter for help. He came over to the kiosk with us and logged in, as we had already done which gave us the same result we previously had. He told us that he couldn't help us. We accepted that and said thank you. He then said, "ya mon." My wife asked him where he was from. He responded, "Jamaica," and she told him we had just returned from Jamaica for a wedding and it was beautiful.

Almost immediately, he got back onto the kiosk and found us seats together. It's amazing what a little rapport did for us. If you can find something in common with someone and strike up a short conversation, you automatically open the door to having a good experience, whether you are the customer or the person in the sales/serving position.

Here are a few simple tips that we used to go beyond average in providing a good customer experience:

1. Always treat people the way you want to be treated. Look at it as if it was your own money being spent and what you would expect to get back. That's what separates good businesspeople from bad businesspeople. You need to have confidence in knowing what you are selling is a good product and well worth the

money. I left a job working as a salesman at a car dealership because the owner was very deceitful and only about making the sale.

2. Be confident but not cocky and never bad-mouth your competition. It's important to be the bigger, more professional person. Remember, the cream always rises to the top and the truth always prevails. People want someone they can trust. Be trustworthy and honest. No one likes dealing with a crooked sales guy or gal.

3. If you're in retail sales, you can get really frustrated with customers wasting your time and telling you stories. But that's how you build relationships. People no longer just want to be a customer; they want to buy from someone they trust. Being a good listener is part of building a friendship. Build your skills to become a better listener.

4. Follow up with your customers and clients after the sale. And when you have a prospecting customer, don't call to upsell them; instead, touch base to see how everything is going. They will think of you the next time they (or their friends or family) want to make another purchase.

5. Never text or check your phone at a meeting (lunch meeting, interview, new account, etc.). If

you are doing business with someone, that is your main priority at that time. Take your Bluetooth off your ear and give them your undivided attention. Checking your phone automatically sends a signal that you have something more important to do and that they are not your #1 priority at that moment.

6. When talking with people at business meetings, parties, or any kind of gatherings, keep the conversation focused on them. No one really wants to hear how well you're doing. The people who brag the most are usually leveraged to the max. A good rule of thumb is to only answer questions that are asked of you and keep the topic on others. People love to talk about themselves.

7. Out-service your competition and be the best at what you do. Our motto "under promise and over deliver," has proven time and time again to be the best form of advertisement while providing excellent customer service. We did this in our dealership and also with partners in our television show. When we were filming with partners, we worked harder and stayed longer than anyone else, which didn't go unnoticed.

8. Welcome competition. Good competition makes you rise to the occasion and in the end, everyone wins.

9. Don't be afraid to take it away. People always want what they can't have. This worked for us so many times in business. I found we averaged better at the dealership and in television partnerships if we took it away. The art of taking it away is to learn how to sell without being so pushy. You can do this easily by changing the focus of the conversation or by not calling someone to the point where you become an annoyance. Another way to take it away is by having two buyers for the same thing so you are not so focused on that one buyer making the purchase. This comes down to you creating a good balance of supply and demand.

10. Believe in yourself and what you are selling. Don't be afraid to go after it, but don't seem desperate. The squeaky wheel always gets the grease.

## Appearance Matters

We all know that appearance matters in today's society, especially when it comes to owning a successful retail store. Potential customers decide whether or not they will shop at your store based on its presentation from the street. If your appearance says, "I'm bankrupt," it won't be long before you will be. It's important to take a look at your business from the outside just as a new customer would. How does your business look from the street? Does it look like a successful business or days away from closing the doors? What is the inside like? Does it look and smell clean? Are your windows clean? Do you have good lighting and signage? How is the appearance of your team?

Cleanliness and organization can be just as important as customer service and cost. It doesn't take a lot of money to sweep and mop the floors or throw on a fresh coat of paint. When we owned our ATV dealership, we would not only work on the outside presentation but also on the inside by painting, dusting, cleaning, and rearranging our inventory and displays. We would also purchase new display racks, posters, and signage on a regular basis so there was always something that appeared to be new and happening. Investing in a great appearance can do wonders for your bottom line.

In retail, good lighting is essential as well as music playing to help break that awkward silence. Have you ever been in a retail store where it's so quiet you could hear a mouse fart? And then to top it off, you have the salesperson sitting behind the counter just grilling you? This makes for a very uncomfortable situation for customers and it won't be long before they move on.

Creating a welcoming atmosphere isn't rocket science, and you should think of it as one of the most important elements of a retail business. This can be important in many other types of businesses too. As we conducted meetings in our production offices for the television show, we thought it was essential to welcome our guests with a friendly presentation. This included things like a welcome sign with their names in the reception area; fresh flowers in the conference room; and having water, coffee, and snacks available. We would also put out a memo to our team a day in advance with notification that we were expecting visitors and we would like them to clean up their work area and dress to impress.

# CHAPTER 10

## Time to MSH! (Powering Through)

It's funny how when you're starting out in business or have a goal and you announce what you're going to do, people say you're "cocky" or "full of yourself." When you finally do achieve a certain level of success, they are the same people who say you got lucky. I hear it all the time, "Boy you sure did get lucky," or "How did you land this job?" They have no clue about everything we went through to get to this point in our life. All they see is what is in front of them. Did you ever hear the phrase "The harder I work, the luckier I get?" That's my life in a nutshell. We've not only worked hard, but we've also learned how to work smart.

So many people are sitting around hoping to win the lottery or inherit a lot of money from a rich relative they didn't know existed. The odds are against you if that's your mindset. I knew I wasn't the luckiest guy in the world when it came to the lottery or just being given anything. If I wanted anything, I had to earn it and make it happen.

Besides the success we achieved with our television show, we experienced a level of success with our

"Keepin' It Real Tour," which we produced for four years, and our very own off-road event, Fisher's ATV Reunion, bringing together 5,000 attendees for six consecutive years.

Over the years, we've also traveled the world and experienced some of the coolest adventures imaginable. We've had the opportunity to work with many well-known celebrities, country music artists, political figures, and NASCAR drivers. None of this happened by chance. It happened because we never looked at anything as impossible.

## Program Your Brain

Did you know that success is 80 percent psychological and only 20 percent doing the work? Remember, your brain is like a computer so you need to program it for success. Some things that helped me to do this were reading lots of self-help and motivational books, listening to many audio books, watching videos and You Tube. With all the interactive media today, tons of this material and information is right at your fingertips. I would highly suggest looking for a few speakers that you really relate to and get hooked up with their seminars, books, videos, and so on.

I wish there was just one key that I could give you to make you successful. Unfortunately, there are many different concepts that make a person successful. For me, the specific keys that helped me the most were staying focused, going beyond average, and being persistent. For you, they may be different but I guarantee that my keys will be helpful to you someday in some way, shape, or form.

Your belief in yourself will always reflect your level of talent. There are so many opportunities for all of us to take advantage of, and your life will be whatever you make of it. I knew that I wasn't put here to sit around and wait for things to happen. I needed to *make* them happen and that's exactly what we did and will continue to do—"MSH" or Make S#!+ Happen!

## If I Can Do It . . .

First, to MSH in your life and business, you have to quit making excuses for yourself and take the words "I can't" out of your vocabulary. You need to have a high level of self-confidence and self-esteem and push on. Don't let fear or procrastination stop you from doing the things you want to do. Those two things are the biggest robbers of success. You will always have critics, no matter how great your idea is. If you allow the critics to control your thinking, they will. But they're just more obstacles put in your path, testing how you overcome life's challenges. Tuning out these negative voices makes you stronger.

Once you get the mindset that no matter what comes your way you are ready and will power through, nothing can stand in your way. And while some challenges and adversities may knock your feet right out from under you, all you have to do is dig deep in your heart and find your way because it's not over as long as you get back up. I'm hoping that by sharing my story, you will be inspired and understand that life is what you make it. If a small town boy who grew up without a dad and mom and graduated 236 out of 236—bottom of my class in high school—and fought every inch of the way to make something of his life, then you can too.

## The Rewards

In our journey to be successful, we've experienced a lot of rewards—some for me personally and some for my family. For one, we get to work together every day and enjoy a life full of adventure. Melissa was never a big dreamer for things in life, but she has a huge heart and loves doing things for other people, especially children. It's cool to know that all of our hard work allows her to do that. I like having nice trucks, a nice house, lots of toys and being able to give back to others.

I feel most thankful that we've been able to give back to my mom and dad. As I mentioned earlier, my grandparents (Dad and Mom) spent their retirement years raising me because my mother (their daughter) passed away in a car accident when I was just ten months old. They helped Melissa and me with babysitting countless times when our kids were younger and we were trying every different business idea under the sun.

As Dad and Mom grew older, they sold their home and moved to an assisted living facility. Eventually my dad was requiring more care than could be provided by the facility they were in. But there wasn't a place for them to go where they could be together because they required different levels of care. This meant they would have to separate and live apart. Now they were married for sixty-eight years at this point, and separating them would have been devastating.

Melissa and I bought the house next to us and remodeled to accommodate them so they could stay together. We were able to hire a staff of helpers and nurses to care for them. They got to spend the next two and a half years together and on December 22, 2011, my dad passed at age ninety-four, and I was there holding his hand. He was not in a nursing home by himself. Because of the sacrifices we made, we were able to do that for them. That's what it's all about!

Over the years we've had a lot of successes and many more failures. Our failures are why we succeeded. How did I overcome so many obstacles with very little education, no contacts, and no money? I knew exactly what I wanted and I went after it. I designed my life the way I wanted it to be, and the law of attraction saw it through. Whatever you tell yourself is exactly what your brain will believe. Henry Ford said it best: "Whether you think you can, or you think you can't—you're right."

## My Formula for Success

My dirt road has been full of ups and downs and lots of twist and turns, but it continues to head in the direction that I envisioned it would. My formula for success:

1. Know what you want.
2. Figure out your plan to get it.
3. Stay focused.
4. Go beyond average.
5. Be persistent.

Every negative or positive event that happens to you was attracted by you; that's all a part of the law of attraction (LOA). When you first learn about the LOA, it may seem kind of crazy until you see it in action. Am I saying it's like magic and will happen right away? No. All I can tell you is that the more I believed in something and saw it crystal clear in my mind and expected it to happen—it did. Sometimes it took weeks, months, or even years but it did eventually come around. I feel things will happen for us and fall into line when we're ready.

## Dreams Do Come True

Sometimes you might be on the verge of something big like a new home, new car, a relationship, or sales deal, and it falls through. Now you might have really wanted this and could see yourself there, but it doesn't happen. This may be because there is something better for you coming your way but you can't see into the future. Be patient. A perfect example of this is when Melissa and I were looking for our dream home. I put our vision of the perfect dream home in front of us all the time. We were going to have a 5,000 square foot home on fifty wooded acres with a big pole barn, and a pond or stream running through the property. It would also have a one-fourth to a half-mile driveway back to our home and would back up against some kind of state forest land.

My wife and I lived in Pennsylvania at the time and looked at several homes in that area over a three-year period. Every house we looked at, we would say this isn't exactly what we want, and we really considered settling on a few. As a matter of fact, we did put a few offers on the table but they always seemed to fall through.

Our television show has taken us all over the country and we've made quite a few long-distance friendships. Our friend from Tennessee recommended looking around Nashville, which is just what we did. It didn't take long to put a contract in on a home but again, it fell through at the last minute because the owner found out who we were and raised the price $25,000 because he figured we would pay it.

We continued our search and probably looked at eighty more houses in a two-month period. We we're ready to call it quits when, on the last day, the next-to-the-last house we looked at really caught our eye. We had our realtor put in an offer, which she assured us they would not agree to, but we put it in anyway. Our realtor called us back two days later and said, "You're never going to believe this, but they took your offer!"

I guess now would be a good time to tell you a little about the home that we bought. We now own a 5,000 square foot home on fifty wooded acres, with a pond, a one-fourth mile driveway, a huge 40 x 40 foot pole barn, plus it backs up to 2,000 acres of Tennessee Wildlife Management land. As I mentioned earlier, this is just what I envisioned and just what we got. This has everything to do with goal setting and is a great example of how the law of attraction works.

Earlier in this book, I made reference to a theory of multiple intelligences written by Howard Gardner, "It's not how smart you are. It's how you are smart." I could see what my life was going to be like, long before I ever came close to getting any of it. It came about because of the relentless pursuit of a dream!

After all the challenges and adversity Melissa and I had in life and our business, I'll never forget the first morning we woke up in our beautiful dream home near Nashville, Tennessee. It was November 1, 2012. This was fall and the leaves were vibrant with color. We had six deer and a turkey feeding right in our front yard. Melissa was looking out the front window at our amazing view across the valley with no other houses in sight. As I brought coffee to her, I noticed she was crying. I said, "What's wrong baby?" She looked at me and said. "I can't believe this is all ours. It's like a dream come true." Did you hear that last part? "It's like a dream come true."

I know this is just the beginning of my story. I've got a lot of miles ahead of me, and I am excited about what my future holds. The road you take is up to you, no one but YOU! So what's programmed in your GPS? Are you ready to MSH?

**For more on Brian Fisher or to book Brian for your next event, visit www.brianfisherspeaks.com.**

# ABOUT THE AUTHOR

Brian Fisher is the host and executive producer of the award-winning television show, *Fisher's ATV World*, which aired nationally on Outdoor Channel for over twelve years and later moved to larger networks such as Discovery's Velocity, Destination America and NBC Sports Network reaching millions more viewers! The show also aired around the world in many other countries and was translated into several different languages. Brian has made a name for himself in outdoor television with his fun personality and "keepin' it real" style.

Brian knows what it takes to be successful. His journey is one of true endurance, but yet relatable to many others on the dirt road toward success. He was not the child born with a silver spoon in his mouth. He was a boy with a burning desire to be successful and a "do whatever it takes" attitude.

Growing up in the small town of Dover, Pennsylvania, Brian graduated high school at the very bottom of his class in 1987. He was ranked 236 out of 236 his senior year and voted "most likely to fail" by many of his teachers and classmates. Brian's dream was to have his own business and be successful.

Brian married his wife, Melissa in 1992, and together they had three wonderful children. Brian worked in the printing industry for twelve years and knows firsthand what hard work is all about. The journey to owning their own business was one of true triumph, complete with ups and downs, twists and turns, many failures, but always with the tenacity to push on toward success. Several business ideas came and went throughout the years, however, giving up was never an option.

Brian and his family shared a love for the outdoors and riding ATVs. This was their way of spending quality family time together. In 1999, Brian Fisher and Melissa started a used ATV dealership, Fisher's ATV World, in the small town of Dover, Pennsylvania. Providing great customer service was key to making their ATV dealership a true success. The first full year in business, their dealership brought in over one million dollars. This growth continued and allowed Brian to push his dream of wanting to host an outdoor television program focused on ATV adventures to the next level. With over 320 million Americans and one out of every nine homes with a motorcycle, ATV, or side by side, surely this would be a hit!

Brian had no television experience and really had no idea of what it would take to pull it all together. He just knew that hard work and perseverance always pays off and had always believed in his heart that you can do anything you put your mind to if you don't give up. The ATV dealership invested $250,000 into the television program to air on Outdoor Channel for the first year before sponsorships started rolling in. Brian made the sales calls himself to major companies to sell them on the idea of partnering with the television show. Brian taught himself when it came to sales and has earned a lot of respect within the industry. His knowledge of business varies from being the customer to working with customers at the dealership and later dealing with corporate clients and advertising agencies for the television show.

Brian has been face to face with many business challenges and adversities throughout his career and now, for the first time, he is ready to share his experiences and knowledge to help others as they pursue their dreams/goals in business and in life.

Brian and his television show, *Fisher's ATV World*, won several awards since first airing in 2002. These awards include sixty-four Bronze Telly Awards and seven Silver Telly Awards from 2004 to 2014. In 2011, *Fisher's ATV World* was honored with the Golden Moose Award for "Best Off-Road Series" on Outdoor Channel.

Brian Fisher has also served as the spokesperson for Progressive ATV Insurance. Other corporate partners include but are not limited to large corporate companies such as Yamaha, Can-Am, Suzuki, Honda, Warn Industries, Carlisle Tire/ ITP, Keystone RV, Tucker Rocky Distribution/Quadboss, and others. Brian is an acclaimed pro rider and has been featured in many national articles including but not limited to *ATVA*, *Dirt Wheels* magazine, *4 Wheel ATV Action* magazine, *ATV Rider* magazine, *RV Business* magazine and many others.

As of January 2015, Brian's adventures for the show have taken him to thirty-nine US states and four different countries. He has also hosted quite a few well-known celebrities as guests on the show. Viewers enjoy Brian's sense of humor and "keepin' it real" style. He quickly became the guy that everyone wanted to go riding with on the weekends.

In 2010, Brian Fisher rolled out the *Fisher's ATV World* "Keepin' It Real" Tour, complete with a tour bus, and traveled to promote trail riding parks, events, and trails around the country for the next several years. He also started a fan club, Fisher's Mud Club and began selling his own line of products to the off-road industry. Brian and his team at *Fisher's ATV World* hosted their very own "off-road" event, Fisher's

ATV Reunion, from 2008 to 2013, bringing together approximately 5,000 attendees each year.

Brian Fisher now lives in Nashville, Tennessee with his wife Melissa and three adult children. They live life to the fullest with no plans of letting off the throttle yet.

If you're ready to make a decision to do whatever it takes, let Brian's story encourage and inspire you to move forward. His lessons in life are hands on—the real deal! He knows challenge and adversity because he has been there, done that! Whether you're looking for some helpful information from a business perspective or something a little more personal, Brian's life lessons give you some things to think about that could change your life forever!

43871912R00103

Made in the USA
Charleston, SC
08 July 2015